AF877815

AVOY PUBLISHING
· Estate Execution & Probate Series ·
· Book 1 of 4 ·

THE EXECUTOR'S PRACTICAL GUIDE

Step-by-Step Instructions for Settling an Estate and Handling Probate

A. Perkins

AVOY PUBLISHING
First Edition · 2026

The Executor's Practical Guide: Step-by-Step Instructions for Settling an Estate and Handling Probate.

First Edition · 2026 · Printed in the United States of America.

Copyright © 2026 by AVOY, LLC. All rights reserved worldwide.

Published in the United States of America by AVOY, LLC ('AVOY Publishing'). AVOY, LLC maintains the worldwide publication and distribution rights to this work.

No part of this publication may be reproduced, stored in a retrieval system, or transmitted in any form or by any means — electronic, mechanical, photocopying, recording, scanning, or otherwise — without the prior written permission of the publisher, except in the case of brief quotations embodied in critical reviews and certain other noncommercial uses permitted by copyright law.

Permissions and editorial inquiries may be directed to ap@avoyhq.com.

Print ISBN (Hardcover): 978-1-969048-95-1

Print ISBN (Paperback): 978-1-969048-94-4

eBook ISBN: 978-1-969048-96-8

Audiobook ISBN: 978-1-969048-97-5

Cover design and interior typography by AVOY, LLC. Typeset in Georgia and presented in the AVOY house style: burgundy and bronze on cream.

Publisher's Cataloging-in-Publication data available upon request.

For the people who say yes

when their family asks —

and learn the job

one careful step at a time.

Being executor is not honorary.

It is the last act of love

you perform for the person who chose you,

and the first act of fairness

you perform for everyone who loved them.

The Executor's Practical Guide

LEGAL NOTICE & DISCLAIMER

◆

This book is for general education. It is not legal, tax, or financial advice. Estate administration is governed by fifty different state codes and by each county's local court rules, and the details change over time. For your situation, work with a licensed attorney in your state.

Thresholds, deadlines, fees, and forms cited in these pages are accurate at the time of writing and will drift. Verify any specific figure against the current state code and local court rule before you act on it.

Names and stories in the case-study vignettes are composites. Any resemblance to real people, families, or estates is coincidental. Reading this book does not create an attorney-client or fiduciary relationship with the author, AVOY, LLC, or anyone else who worked on it.

Neither the author nor AVOY, LLC accepts liability for losses arising from reliance on this book.

By reading on, you accept these terms.

CONTENTS

HOW TO READ THIS BOOK

◆

The Executor's Practical Guide is organized in five movements, in roughly the order you will face the work. Read straight through, or flip to whichever chapter answers the question in front of you right now.

Where to Start

Pick whichever describes you:

- **A death just happened and you do not know what to do today.** Start with Chapter 1 — the first 24 to 72 hours, in order. Then come back to Chapter 2 when you can sit down with coffee.
- **You were named in the will and are deciding whether to accept.** Start with Chapter 2 — what the job actually is, what it is not, and how to decline cleanly if you need to.
- **You have been appointed and the work has started.** Skim Chapters 1–2, then read Chapters 3–6 in order — finding the will, securing assets, sending notices, handling debts.
- **You are in the middle and overwhelmed.** Jump to Chapter 11 — the month-by-month timeline. Find where you are this month, then read the matching earlier chapter.

- **You are trying to wrap up and close the estate.** Read Chapters 9 and 12 — distribution, then the final closing checklist.

Reading Conventions

Three visual conventions repeat through the book:

- **KEY POINT callouts (amber).** The most important structural facts in each chapter. Read these if you are skim-reading.
- **DO THIS NOW callouts (amber, action language).** A concrete step you can take this week before you keep reading.
- **WHAT IS AN EXECUTOR? definition box (olive).** Plain-language definitions of legal terms the first time they appear.

Tables and figures are labeled "Table X.X" and "Figure X.X" and integrated into the text. Every technical term is also defined in the Glossary at the back.

What's at the Back of This Book

Roughly the back third is reference material. Come back to it when you need it:

- **Conclusion.** What you now know about doing this work well.

- **Reader FAQ.** Common questions organized by stage — first weeks, middle months, closing — each cross-referenced to the chapter that covers it.
- **Glossary of Estate Terms.** Plain-English definitions of every technical word in the book.
- **Bibliography & Reference Guide.** Statutory sources, treatises, online portals for readers who want to dig deeper.
- **About the Publisher and About the Author.** Short notes on AVOY and the author.
- **Twelve Appendices (A–L).** Executor at a Glance · State Probate Threshold Map · First-Sixty-Days Checklist · Common Forms · Sample Letter to Beneficiaries · Annotated Reading List · Twelve-Month Calendar · Family Communication Framework · Subject Index · Quick-Start Guide · Chapter-by-Chapter Summary · The Complete AVOY Library.

Now to the book itself.

PREFACE

The first thing to know about being executor is that almost no one feels ready for it. You do not apply. You do not train. You get called by a lawyer, or find your name in a will, or — more often than you would think — find out at the funeral when someone hands you a stack of papers.

> **WHAT IS AN EXECUTOR?**
>
> The executor (or personal representative, or administrator — same job, different state names) is the person legally responsible for closing out a deceased person's finances. Three big jobs: find what they owned and owed, pay the debts and taxes, and distribute what's left to the people the will names. You answer to the court, the beneficiaries, and any creditor. The estate comes first — not you. That's the whole frame.

Then you say yes. Because saying yes feels like loyalty. Because the person who chose you is no longer here to choose someone else. Because nobody else volunteered.

The good news: most of the job is doable by anyone who can follow a checklist and keep written records. It runs about two hundred to four hundred hours over nine to fifteen months — spread out, mostly phone calls, envelopes, and notes.

The bad news: nobody hands you the playbook. Courts have forms but not explanations. Lawyers charge by the hour.

The internet is a mix of the merely incomplete and the actively misleading.

This book is the playbook. Twelve chapters in roughly the order things happen. First 72 hours, first 30 days, the heavy middle, distribution, closing. By the end, the estate is closed and you have done one of the more difficult things adult life asks of anyone.

Read with patience. The work rewards it.

INTRODUCTION

Why This Book Exists

◆

Why This Book Exists

Most American families will go through the executor's job at least once. Often two or three times in an adult lifetime — for a parent, then a spouse, then an aunt or a sibling.

Each time, the family member who gets the job is usually doing it for the first time. Each time, they figure out the same things the last family had to figure out. Each time, the early weeks are a fog of grief, paperwork, and unanswered questions.

There are four reasons this book exists:

- Most executors have never done it before — and have to learn the job in grief, on a deadline, while answering condolence calls.
- Most writing about executors is either a legal treatise (too technical) or a consumer pamphlet ("hire a lawyer" and nothing else). This book sits in the gap between them.
- The shape of the job has not changed in fifty years. The work itself is largely the same from estate to estate. What

is missing is a plain-language guide that walks you through it in order.

- The estate runs faster, cheaper, and easier when the executor knows what is coming. That information should not be a secret.

Who This Book Is For

If any of these describes you, this book is for you:

- An executor in week one, holding a will and a stack of unopened mail.
- An administrator without a will, just appointed by the court.
- A spouse or adult child trying to help a grieving family member who said yes to the job.
- A beneficiary who wants to know what is happening with the estate.
- Anyone planning their own affairs who wants to make life easier for whoever serves as their executor someday.

What You Will Know When You Finish

By the last chapter you will know, with practical confidence:

- What to do in the first 24, 48, and 72 hours.
- What the executor's job actually is — and what it is not.
- Where to find the will when you cannot find the will.

- Which assets go through probate and which skip it entirely.
- How to secure the house, the bank accounts, the investments, the business — and which to leave alone.
- Who to notify, in what order, and what to actually say.
- How the creditor process works, and what beneficiaries are not on the hook for.
- How to manage the estate's money while the case is open.
- When to hire a lawyer and when to do it yourself.
- How to distribute fairly, with documentation that protects you.
- The eleven recurring mistakes — and the cure for each.
- A clean month-by-month timeline from death to discharge.
- The 20-item closing checklist that ends the job legally and emotionally.

This is not legal advice. It is not tax advice. It is a foundation. With it, you will be in a position to ask better questions, recognize bad advice when you hear it, and make better decisions about a job that arrived in your life uninvited.

That is the value of a book like this.

Let's begin.

PART 1

CLARITY

What this job is, and what to do in the first seventy-two hours.

CHAPTER 1

What Happens First (The First 24–72 Hours)

Chapter at a Glance

- What to do in the first 24 hours, the next 24, and the third 24.
- How to confirm the death legally (pronouncement vs death certificate).
- What to lock down at the house and what to leave alone.
- Why you should not yet call the bank, the employer, or post the obituary.
- The five things that should be true by the end of day three.

Someone you love has died. You've been told you're the executor — or the personal representative, or the administrator. Different states use different words for the same job.

What it means is this: you're the person responsible for closing out their financial life.

That responsibility starts now. Not when you visit a lawyer. Not when the probate court calls. Now. In the first seventy-two hours, choices get made that will either make the next year smoother or harder. This chapter walks through what those choices are, in the order they need to happen.

You don't have to do all of it yourself. You just have to make sure it gets done — by you, by a family member, by the funeral home, by a lawyer when you bring one in.

> **KEY POINT**
>
> In the first 72 hours, your job is not to administer the estate. Your job is to (1) confirm the death legally, (2) lock down the home and the obvious assets, and (3) put your hands on the important paperwork. Everything else can wait a week.

Hour 0 to 24 — Confirm and Notify

When someone dies at home or in a hospital, a medical professional — the hospice nurse, the attending physician, the paramedic — pronounces the death. They issue a pronouncement of death. That's not the same as the death certificate. The death certificate comes later, usually within a few days, signed by the physician who certifies the cause.

Your job in this window is small and specific:

- Call the immediate family. Personally. Not by text, not on Facebook.
- Call the funeral home you want to use. If your loved one pre-arranged a funeral, the contract is usually in their

important-papers file.

- If the death was at home, the funeral home will arrange the transfer of the body. You don't need to be there if it's too painful.
- If they were a veteran, mention that to the funeral home. There are benefits — a flag, military honors, a burial allowance — that flow through them.

Hold off on the public announcement. Don't post on Facebook yet. Don't publish the obituary yet. Don't call the bank, the employer, or Social Security yet. Those things matter, but they're not for day one — and posting too early creates problems we'll get into in Chapter 5.

Hour 24 to 48 — Secure the Home

If your loved one lived alone, the home is now empty. That sounds obvious. What's less obvious is the consequence.

An empty home with a recently deceased occupant is a target. Sometimes for outright theft. Often for well-meaning relatives who "just want a keepsake." And almost always for boring problems that get bigger if no one is checking — utility issues, a leaking pipe, a stack of mail growing on the porch that signals to everyone the house is empty.

Within the first 48 hours, do these things, in order:

1. Lock every door and every window. Walk the perimeter. Make a list of anyone you know was given a key — neighbors, dog walkers, cleaners — so you can ask for the keys back later. (Don't go retrieve them yet. We've got a checklist for that in Chapter 4.)

2. Bring the mail inside. Don't forward anything yet. Just collect what's piled up and put it in one box, unopened.

3. Check the fridge and freezer. Throw out anything that will spoil. The smell of rotting groceries is a small thing today that becomes a big thing in week three.

4. Set the thermostat to a sensible temperature — around 55–60°F in winter, around 78°F in summer. Low enough to save on utilities, high enough to keep pipes from freezing or humidity from wrecking the walls.

5. Photograph every room. Wide shots first. Then open every closet and every cabinet and shoot what's inside, in place. This is your starting inventory. If someone later asks where the silver candlesticks went, you have a picture.

6. Find and secure: the will, the keys, the wallet or purse (with cards intact), any visible jewelry, any cash on the premises. Put them somewhere you can re-access — a safe deposit box, a locked drawer, your own home. Make a note of where.

Hour 48 to 72 — Save the Paperwork

By now, the funeral is being arranged. Family has been told. The home is locked. What you do next will determine how easy or hard the next twelve months are.

Round up the following and put them in one folder or one labeled box:

- The will — the original if you can find it. (Copies usually aren't good enough for probate.)
- Trust documents, if there's a trust.
- Recent bank statements — last three months will do for now.
- Recent brokerage and retirement statements.
- Insurance policies — life, home, auto, health.
- Mortgage paperwork and any loan paperwork.
- Tax returns for the last two or three years.
- Vehicle titles.
- Social Security card.
- Birth certificate, marriage certificate, divorce papers if any, military discharge (the DD-214) for veterans.
- Passport.
- Address book or phone contacts.
- Pre-arranged funeral contract, cemetery deed, prepaid burial paperwork.

Can't find the will? Don't panic. Most of the time it shows up. Chapter 3 walks through the places wills usually live and what to do if no original ever turns up.

By the end of seventy-two hours, here's what should be true:

1. Immediate family has been told personally.
2. The funeral home has the body, and arrangements are underway.
3. The home is locked, secured, and photographed.
4. The fridge is cleared, the thermostat is set, the mail is being collected.
5. The will and the most important documents are in one place, and you have them.

That's the whole first-72-hour assignment. You haven't opened a probate case yet. You haven't hired a lawyer yet. You haven't called the bank. You did five things, and those five things are the foundation everything else rests on.

KEY POINT

DO THIS NOW — Before you read Chapter 2, write down (on paper or in a note on your phone): where the will is, where the keys are, where the wallet is, the funeral home contact, and who's been told. This is your first official act as executor. From here on, everything is documented.

What This Looks Like in Practice

Margaret got the call at 7:14 on a Tuesday morning. Her father had died overnight at the hospice facility. The hospice nurse had already pronounced the death. The funeral home Margaret's father had pre-arranged with would arrive within two hours.

By 9:00 she had called her two siblings personally. By 10:30 she had driven the forty minutes to her father's apartment. By noon the locks were checked, the mail was inside, the thermostat was at sixty-five, and the refrigerator was empty.

She had also photographed every room in the apartment — wide shots first, then every drawer and closet — and put the will, the keys, and his wallet into a single folder she'd brought with her.

She did not yet call his bank. She did not post on Facebook. She did not start telling the credit-card companies. She stopped at her brother's house, sat on his porch, and cried for an hour. Then she went home and slept for fourteen hours.

When she woke up Wednesday morning, the worst seventy-two hours of executor work were already 80% done.

What This Chapter Has Said

Notes from Real Estates

Three things people consistently underestimate about the first 72 hours.

One: how many death certificates you'll need. Eight to ten feels like a lot. It isn't. Every bank, every brokerage, every insurance company, the Social Security office, the DMV, the IRS, the credit bureaus, and the title company on the house will each demand one. Some will return them. Most won't.

If you order too few, you'll end up making a second trip to the vital-records office and waiting another two weeks. Order ten the first time. The cost is small ($10–$25 each in most states) and the time savings is real.

Two: how fast identity thieves move. Within 24–48 hours of an obituary publication, identity thieves harvest names and dates of birth and try to open credit accounts. Get the credit-bureau notices in before the obituary runs. The bureaus mark the file as deceased within a couple of days, and the new-account attempts get blocked automatically.

Without that step, you may spend months untangling fraud.

Three: what to do about the deceased's phone. If they had a smartphone, the phone is often the gateway to digital assets, two-factor authentication, photos, and contacts. Don't reset it. Don't take it back to the carrier. Charge it, keep it in your possession, and figure out the digital side carefully over the next month.

A phone that's been factory-reset has lost everything; a phone that's been preserved is one of the most useful tools you have.

Patterns That Repeat

Three patterns we see almost every time, in the first 72 hours, regardless of the family or the wealth level.

Pattern: the immediate sibling argument

Within 48 hours of a parent's death, two siblings will almost certainly disagree about something specific — the funeral arrangements, the contents of a particular drawer, who should hold the keys, whether to call the lawyer today or wait until next week. The disagreement is rarely about the specific thing.

It's about the relationship patterns the family has had for forty years, surfacing now under stress.

The executor's job is not to resolve those patterns. Your job is to make a single, narrow decision: what gets done now to secure the estate. If the locks need changing, change them. If the will needs locating, locate it. The family dynamics will keep. Don't try to fix in week one what hasn't been fixable in four decades.

Pattern: the well-meaning relative who "helps" too much

A cousin will offer to "start going through Mom's papers." An aunt will offer to "sort the clothes for donation." A nephew will offer to "start emptying the garage."

Say thank you and decline. Nothing gets sorted, donated, or emptied until after the inventory is complete. The well-meaning helpers are not bad people. They are people who are uncomfortable with grief and want to be useful. Their help, in week one, costs you the documented baseline you'll need later. Redirect their energy: meals, transportation, time with the immediate family.

Not the physical sorting of the estate.

Pattern: the first 72 hours feel longer than they are

Figure 1.1

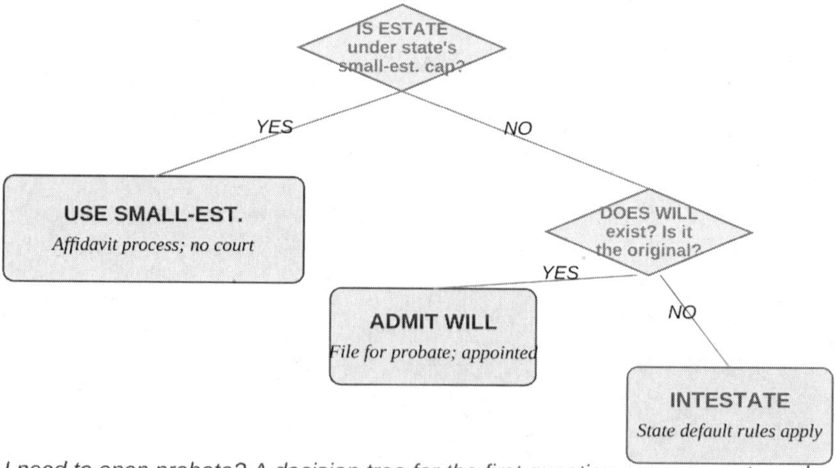

Do I need to open probate? A decision tree for the first question every executor asks.

Time stretches in the first few days. Everything feels urgent. Nothing actually is, beyond what we've listed in this chapter. If you find yourself drafting tax-return questions on day three, you've gotten ahead of yourself. Slow down. Five things in three days. Sleep when you can.

The probate court will open Monday whether or not you have everything figured out today.

The first 72 hours aren't about running the estate. They're about confirming the death, locking down the home, and saving the paperwork. Confirm through the funeral home. Lock up the house. Put the will and the important documents in one place. Five things. Three days. Everything else can wait a week.

CHAPTER 2

Understanding Your Role as Executor

Chapter at a Glance

- The executor's job in three stages — find, pay, distribute.
- The one rule that governs everything you do (and what happens when you break it).
- What the job is not — and the people you do not have to answer to.
- Whether you can get paid for your time (yes, usually).
- How to decline before appointment, or step down after, without burning bridges.

Now that the house is locked and the will is in your hands, let's talk about what you've actually agreed to do.

Being executor isn't honorary. It's not a thank-you note. It's a real job, with real obligations to real people, and real consequences when those obligations aren't met.

Understanding the shape of the job — before you start doing it — is the difference between an estate that closes in nine to fifteen months and an estate that drags on for three years and ends in a family lawsuit.

> **KEY POINT**
>
> Being named executor is an offer, not a sentence. You can turn it down before the court formally appoints you. You can even step down after appointment if you really need to (it's messier). The choice to serve should be made with eyes open.

What the Job Actually Is

Boiled down, it has three stages:

1. Figure out everything they owned and everything they owed.
2. Pay the debts and the taxes, in the order the law says.
3. Give what's left to whoever the will names, in the amounts the will says.

Around those three stages are smaller jobs — filing tax returns, telling creditors, publishing required notices, reporting to the court, handling challenges, managing money during the months it takes to close. Each gets its own chapter. But the three-stage frame is the whole structure. Keep it in mind and the day-to-day stops feeling random.

The Big Rule: You Work for the Estate, Not Yourself

There's a fancy legal name for this — "fiduciary duty" — but the idea is simple. As executor, you have to put the estate first. Not your own interests. Not your favorite sibling's interests. The estate's.

Practically, that means:

- Treat all the beneficiaries the same. You can't favor your sister because you like her better.
- No self-dealing. You can't sell your mother's car to yourself for less than it's worth, even if you'd have inherited it anyway.
- Keep estate money separate from your money. The estate gets its own bank account. Money does not flow through your personal account, ever.
- Track every dollar in and every dollar out. You'll show the court and the beneficiaries the full picture at the end.
- Don't sit on the estate forever. "Reasonable" depends on how complicated it is, but estates that drift for years invite trouble.

Most executors who get in trouble don't do it on purpose. They do it by accident — by mixing money, by not writing things down, by promising a beneficiary something that doesn't pan out. The fixes are administrative, not moral. We'll go through them.

What the Job Is Not

Just as important — what you're not on the hook for:

- You don't owe the deceased's debts. The estate pays them. If the estate doesn't have enough money, most debts go unpaid and creditors get nothing. You do not write a check from your own account.

• You're not the family therapist. People will have feelings about the deceased, about each other, about the will. You can listen. It's not your job to renegotiate the will to make everyone happy.

• You're not the family lawyer. You'll probably hire one (more on when in Chapter 8), but you do not personally give legal advice to anyone.

• You're not on call 24/7. The cousin who texts at midnight about the silverware can wait until morning. This is a project, not an emergency room.

Who You Actually Answer To

Three audiences. That's it.

1. The probate court. They appointed you. They can also un-appoint you.
2. The beneficiaries named in the will. They have a right to know what's going on and to see the books at the end.
3. The creditors. Until the claim window closes, anyone the deceased owed money to gets a fair shot at presenting their claim.

Notice who's not on this list. The deceased's friends. The neighbors. Cousins who weren't named in the will. Distant relatives. The family pastor. You can talk to any of them out of courtesy, but you have no legal obligation, and over-talking with the wrong audience tends to create problems.

Keep your required communication to the court, the beneficiaries, and the creditors.

You're Allowed to Get Paid

Most states let executors take a fee from the estate. The amount depends on state law and on what the will says. Some wills name a flat dollar amount or a percentage. Others leave it to the state's default rules. Family members named as executors often waive the fee as a gesture; non-family executors usually accept it.

If you plan to take a fee, decide early, track your hours, and tell the beneficiaries before the final accounting. Surprise executor fees in the final accounting are one of the top causes of family fights over the estate.

> **KEY POINT**
>
> DO THIS NOW — Before you accept, ask yourself three things: (1) Do I have the time? Estates take 200–400 hours over nine to fifteen months. (2) Can I say no to family pressure when I need to? (3) Am I willing to write things down — every decision, every dollar? If any answer is no, think hard about declining. The next section tells you how.

How to Walk Away

If you decide not to do this, what you do depends on whether the court has already appointed you.

Before appointment: you file a renunciation with the probate court. The will usually names a backup; if not, the court picks someone — typically a beneficiary, a family member, or a professional administrator. The renunciation is a short, one-paragraph filing. The form is usually on the court's website.

After appointment: you file a petition to resign and ask the court to put someone else in. Slower and slightly messier, but it's a real procedure that courts handle all the time.

Say why you're stepping down (time, health, family conflict — anything honest), give a partial accounting through the date you're stepping down, and the next person in line takes over.

Declining isn't a betrayal of the person who named you. Serving badly is. If you can't serve well, decline.

What This Looks Like in Practice

Robert had been named as executor of his aunt's estate. She had no children, and Robert was her closest nephew. The will left half her estate to a Catholic charity and half divided among five nieces and nephews — including Robert himself.

Robert quickly realized his cousin Lisa was unhappy with the split. Lisa had cared for the aunt during her final two years and felt she deserved more than her one-fifth share. She called Robert weekly to argue this.

She wanted him to "renegotiate" with the charity, or to redirect part of the charity's share to her, or to take some of his own share and give it to her informally.

Robert listened. Then he said: "The will says what it says. As executor, I'm not allowed to change it. The charity's share is the charity's share. Your share is your share. If you want to challenge the will formally, you can talk to a probate attorney about that — but I can't do it."

It was an uncomfortable conversation. It was also the right one. Six months later, when the estate closed, the charity got what it was owed, the five nieces and nephews each got what they were owed, and Robert was discharged from his role without a lawsuit. Lisa was still angry. Lisa had also been angry before her aunt died.

Robert hadn't created that. He simply hadn't let it bend the work.

What This Chapter Has Said

Notes from Real Estates

A few things about the executor's role that get clearer after you've actually been one.

The job is more about saying no than yes. Most of what executors do well is decline gracefully. Decline the early request for a specific item. Decline to renegotiate the will. Decline to take a sibling's side. Decline to rush the timeline.

The yeses — opening the account, filing the paperwork, signing the checks — are the easy part.

The work is in the noes.

Compensation is almost never the issue people make it. Most family executors waive their fee. Most non-family executors charge a fair fee documented up front. Where compensation goes wrong is when it's a surprise — when the final accounting shows an executor fee that wasn't disclosed and wasn't expected. Decide early. Communicate early. Document the hours.

The conversation gets harder the longer it's deferred.

The first family fight is the one you didn't see coming. Sometimes it's about money. More often it's about respect — being heard, being included, being treated fairly. A weekly check-in email to all the beneficiaries prevents most of these. It's not the content; it's the consistency. Show up reliably and most of the conflict never starts.

Patterns That Repeat

Pattern: "the will is unfair"

At some point in the first month, one beneficiary will tell you the will is unfair. Sometimes they're right. Sometimes they're not. Either way, it is not your problem to solve.

You are not the author of the will. You did not negotiate its terms. You did not influence the deceased's decisions. You are executing what was decided by the person who is no longer here to be questioned. If a beneficiary wants to challenge the will formally — that's their right.

There is a legal procedure (the will contest) and they can hire counsel and pursue it. Until they do, you carry out what the document says.

Pattern: the executor who keeps saying yes

Figure 2.1

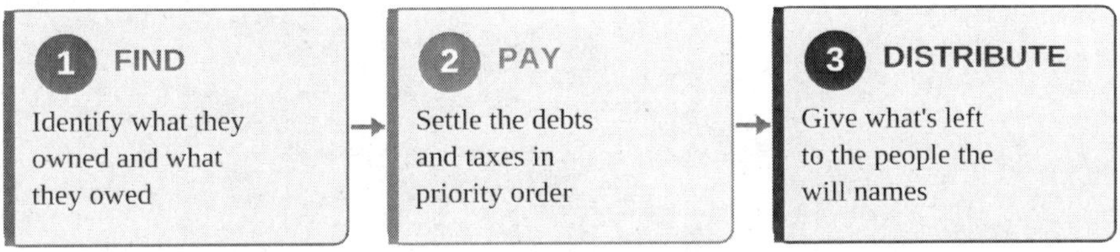

The executor's three jobs — find what was owned and owed, pay debts and taxes, distribute what's left.

Executors who get into trouble usually do so by saying yes too often. Yes to the early distribution request. Yes to the small favor for one beneficiary. Yes to skipping the formal notice because "we know who the creditors are." Each yes feels like generosity in the moment. Each one is a brick in the wall of personal liability.

The default answer in estate administration is no — or more accurately, "not yet." Not yet to distributions. Not yet to specific items. Not yet to anything that hasn't been documented, valued, and authorized. The yes comes at the end, when everything has been done in order.

The executor's job is a three-stage operation — find, pay, distribute — bound by one big rule: put the estate first. You answer to the court, the beneficiaries, and the creditors. Not to everyone with an opinion. You can get paid. You can decline. The rest of this book is the details.

PART 2

PROCESS

How the work actually gets done — finding the documents, locking down the assets, telling the right people, and dealing with what they still owed.

CHAPTER 3

Locating the Will and Key Documents

Chapter at a Glance

- The six places wills usually live (and the order to search them).
- What to do when the original cannot be found.
- The supporting documents that matter as much as the will.
- Why the original beats a copy, and how to handle the missing-original case.
- How to organize what you find so the next eight months go faster.

In a perfect world, the will is in a clearly labeled envelope in the desk drawer, with a copy at the lawyer's office and everything else stacked neatly next to it.

In real life, the will is in a fireproof safe nobody else knows the combination to. Or in a safe deposit box at a bank branch nobody remembers. Or — alarmingly often — nowhere anyone can find.

This chapter walks through where wills usually live, how to search for one without losing your mind, what to do if the original never turns up, and which other papers matter most for what's coming next.

> **KEY POINT**
>
> The original will, not a copy, is what the probate court usually needs. In most states, a copy can be used only with extra proof that the original existed and wasn't deliberately destroyed — and that adds months to probate. Find the original if you can.

The Six Places Wills Usually Live

Roughly in order of how often we find them:

1. A fireproof safe or lockbox at home. If you can find the safe but not the combination, a locksmith can usually open it in a day for $150–$300. Have a witness with you when it's opened, and document the moment.

2. A safe deposit box at the bank. Tricky: in most states the bank can't let you into the box without either a court order, or a key plus death certificate plus proof you're family or executor, or every co-renter present. Some states allow a limited "will retrieval" peek. Call the bank and ask.

3. The estate lawyer's office. Lots of lawyers hold the original after preparing it, especially for wills from before 2010. Look at the deceased's contacts, recent check registers, and email for a lawyer's name.

4. A home filing cabinet, in a folder marked "Important Papers" or "Estate" or sometimes just "Personal." Check the bottom drawer first — important things tend to sink down as new files pile on top.

5. The state's will registry, in states that have one. About a third of states let people register their will with the secretary of state or a court. The fee is small.

6. With a trusted family member. If you don't have the will, ask the immediate family.

If the Original Doesn't Turn Up

Two paths, depending on how thorough you've been.

If it's been less than two weeks: keep looking. Most missing wills show up. Check the car. Check the work desk if there was one. Check storage units. Check the deceased's email and cloud storage for photographed paperwork. Photos of important documents emailed to oneself are increasingly common.

If a real search has come up empty:

- **File a copy, if you have one.** Most states allow probate of a copy with affidavits showing the original existed and wasn't intentionally torn up. The drafting attorney, witnesses, or family who saw the original can sign.

- **File intestate, if there's no copy either.** "Intestate" just means "no will." The state has default rules for who inherits when there's no will. We get into them in Chapter 9.

What Else You Need Besides the Will

The will is the headline. These supporting papers are the rest of the file:

- **Trust documents** — if there's a living trust, the trust controls whatever was titled in it. Many people use a will and a trust together (the will catches anything that didn't make it into the trust).
- **Beneficiary forms** — for retirement accounts (401(k), IRA), life insurance, transfer-on-death accounts. These skip the will entirely and go straight to whoever's named. They matter a lot.
- **Powers of attorney** — financial and medical. These ended at death, but the paper trail can be useful.
- **Living wills / advance directives** — same. File for the record.
- **Recent tax returns** — federal and state, last two or three years. The tax preparer's contact info is usually on the cover page.
- **Account statements** — bank, brokerage, retirement. The most recent ones are enough for now.

- **Deeds and titles** — for the home, for any other real estate, for vehicles.
- **Insurance policies** — life, home, auto, umbrella.
- **Loan paperwork** — mortgage, home equity line, car loans, personal loans, business loans.
- **Personal documents** — Social Security card, Medicare card, military discharge (DD-214), passport, birth and marriage certificates.

> **WHAT'S A POUR-OVER WILL?**
>
> A pour-over will is a short will whose main job is to catch anything that wasn't put into the living trust before death and "pour it over" into the trust during probate. People who use a trust as their main estate plan often have one of these as a safety net for things they bought late or forgot to retitle.

Originals or Copies?

The will: original, if you can. Copy with affidavits, if you have to.

Everything else: copies are usually fine. Courts and banks will take good photocopies of trust documents, beneficiary forms, deeds, tax returns.

One exception: the death certificate. You'll need certified copies — the official ones with a raised seal. Order at least eight to ten through the funeral home or the state vital-records office. Each bank will demand one and most won't give it back.

Get Organized

By the end of this chapter, you should have:

1. The will (original or credible copy with a plan to authenticate).
2. Trust agreement and any amendments, if there's a trust.
3. A folder of beneficiary designations.
4. A folder of account statements.
5. A folder of insurance and loan documents.
6. A folder of real estate and vehicle titles.
7. Personal documents (SSN, passport, birth and marriage certificates, military papers).
8. Tax returns and the tax preparer's contact info.

Label every folder. Put them all in one place you can re-access. We'll come back to them throughout the rest of the book.

> **KEY POINT**
>
> DO THIS NOW — If the will is at the lawyer's office or in a safe deposit box, get it into your hands this week. Probate can't start until the court has the original in front of it. Every week of delay in getting it adds a week to the timeline.

What This Looks Like in Practice

Three days after his mother died, James could not find the will. He had checked the desk, the filing cabinet, the bedroom dresser. Nothing.

He called his sister, who had no idea either. He called his mother's longtime accountant, who told him their mother had used an estate-planning attorney named Sheila Park about twelve years ago. James called Sheila Park's office. They still had the original.

Sheila brought the will to James the following Tuesday, along with a folder of supporting documents she'd kept for his mother — a trust agreement James hadn't known existed, the beneficiary forms for his mother's IRA, and the deed to the family home held in the trust's name.

Without those, James would have spent six months reconstructing an estate plan that was sitting in a filing cabinet on the other side of town. With them, he was able to identify what passed through probate (very little — most was titled in the trust) and what skipped it entirely. He filed for probate in week 2.

His mother's affairs closed in seven months.

What This Chapter Has Said

Notes from Real Estates

Three things about finding the will and the other documents.

The estate-planning attorney is the most underused resource in the first month. If the deceased used one, that lawyer often has not just the will but also the trust documents, the beneficiary forms, contact info for the CPA, and notes from the most recent planning conversation. Call them in week 1.

Most are gracious — they understood this day was coming when they did the original work.

The safe-deposit box deserves a specific call. Most states have a procedure for retrieving the will from a safe-deposit box even when you don't have the key — but the procedure varies. Some states allow limited "will-retrieval" access where the bank's representative removes only the will and reseals the box pending full court authorization.

Others require court order before anyone opens the box. Call the bank's deceased-account specialist in week 1 and ask what their procedure is. It usually takes one phone call and a copy of the death certificate to get the conversation moving.

Digital wills are becoming common but not legally clean. About half the states now recognize fully electronic wills (signed digitally, witnessed digitally, stored in a platform like Trust & Will or Notarize). The other half do not.

If the only "will" you can find is a PDF in the deceased's cloud storage, talk to a probate attorney before filing it — the answer to whether it's valid depends on the state, on the specific platform used, and on the witness procedure followed at execution. Many electronic wills are valid; some are not; very few are easy.

The beneficiary forms are often more important than the will. A 401(k) with a named beneficiary, a life insurance policy with a named beneficiary, a payable-on-death account — these skip the will entirely and go straight to whoever's named on the form. If the form is outdated (still naming an ex-spouse, for example), the form controls.

The current spouse's surprise about this is a real and common pain. The form is what it is, and the executor cannot change it. Find every beneficiary form in week 1 or 2, and contact each custodian to confirm who's currently designated.

Patterns That Repeat

Pattern: the will is in the lawyer's office and no one knows which lawyer

When you can't find an estate-planning attorney's name, check four places in this order: the deceased's check register from the past five years (look for attorney names); the deceased's email inbox (search "will," "trust," "attorney," "estate plan"); the deceased's smartphone contacts (often filed under "lawyer" or "attorney"); and the local bar association's lawyer-referral service (call and ask whether they know of representation by the deceased).

About 80% of the time, one of those four finds the lawyer. The remaining 20% — when the deceased used a lawyer who has since retired or died, or when there was no estate-planning attorney — typically resolves with a thorough physical search of the home or with filing under intestate-succession rules.

Pattern: digital documents the family didn't know existed

Increasingly, the will exists as a PDF the deceased emailed to themselves, or as a Dropbox file, or as a scanned image saved to iCloud. Before declaring the will lost, check the cloud.

Figure 3.1

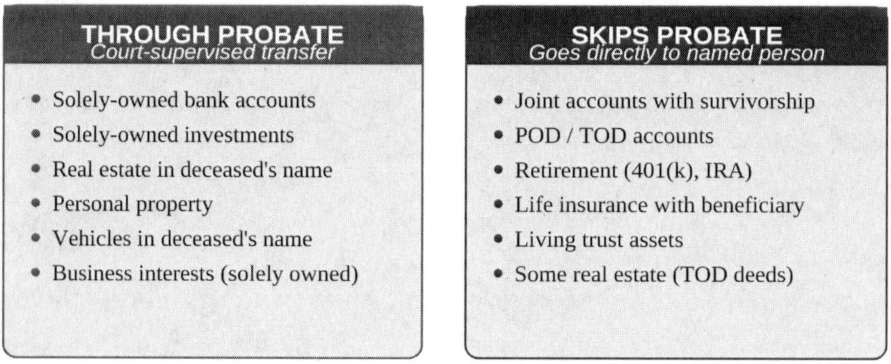

Two kinds of property — what goes through probate, and what skips it entirely.

But: don't log into the deceased's email or cloud storage without going through the provider's deceased-user process. Logging in directly can trigger auto-lock or auto-deletion under the provider's terms of service. Each major provider (Google, Apple, Microsoft) has a specific procedure for next-of-kin access. Follow it.

Wills usually live in one of six places. If the original's missing, you either file a copy with backup proof or proceed as if there's no will. Around the will, the file should include the trust documents, beneficiary forms, account statements, insurance, loans, deeds, titles, personal documents, and tax returns. Organize it now.

The next eight months will be easier for it.

CHAPTER 4

Securing Assets and Property Immediately

Chapter at a Glance

- The difference between securing assets and taking ownership.
- What to do at the house, with vehicles, with bank accounts.
- Why joint accounts and POD/TOD accounts behave differently.
- How to handle business interests and personal property.
- The digital assets that can be permanently lost if mishandled.

An asset that's been secured can't be lost, stolen, drained, or quietly walked off with by a well-meaning relative.

An asset that hasn't been secured can be all four. Often within the first month.

This chapter is about what to lock down, in what order, before the rest of the estate work starts. Speed matters less than thoroughness. You don't have to do all of this in week one. You should be done by the end of week two.

> **KEY POINT**
>
> Securing assets isn't the same as taking ownership. Until the court appoints you (which can take 30–90 days), you don't have legal authority to sell or distribute anything. What you do have is the authority — and the duty — to protect the estate from loss. That starts immediately.

The House

Beyond what Chapter 1 covered:

1. **Change the locks** if the deceased gave out a lot of keys. Or put a keypad lock on the main door. A locksmith runs $80–$200 for a rekey. Log the cost.

2. **Keep the alarm running** if there was one. Call the alarm company, tell them you're the executor, and either keep monitoring active (the estate pays) or pause it. No alarm? Consider a temporary one if the place is in a sketchy neighborhood or will sit empty for a month.

3. **Forward the mail to your address**, or have a neighbor grab it daily. Mail with checks, statements, and bills will keep coming. Capturing it matters. USPS will forward for a deceased person; you'll need a death certificate and proof of executor status (which you may not have yet — in the meantime, pick it up in person).

4. **Tell the closest two or three neighbors.** Give them your phone number. Cheap insurance.

5. **Cancel newspaper delivery, milk delivery, anything that piles up on the porch.** A growing stack signals "nobody home."

6. **Don't turn off the utilities.** The house still needs power for HVAC, water for the pipes, gas for heat. Shutoffs come later, when the place is sold or transferred.

Vehicles

- Take the keys. Park the car in a garage or driveway, not on the street.
- Keep the insurance going. Don't cancel the auto policy yet — if the car gets hit or stolen while you're holding it, you want coverage. Tell the insurer the policyholder has died.
- Watch the registration. If it expires during administration, renew it. The estate pays.
- Take photos — outside, inside, the odometer reading.

Bank Accounts and Investments

The most asked-about category, so let's be specific:

- **Don't withdraw money.** Not with the debit card. Not even for funeral expenses. The moment of death freezes the accounts legally — using them after that is technically theft, even if you mean well.

- **Don't deposit money either.** Tempting when a Social Security check arrives — but Social Security claws back payments for months after death. Depositing those creates a different problem.
- **Do tell the banks.** Once you're appointed, you'll open an estate account (Chapter 7) and consolidate everything. Until then, the existing accounts sit untouched.
- **Joint accounts are different.** If an account was titled jointly "with right of survivorship," it transfers to the surviving owner immediately at death — outside probate, outside the estate. The survivor just brings a death certificate to the bank.
- **Payable-on-death (POD) accounts skip probate too.** Whoever's named brings the death certificate and ID, and the bank hands it over.

POD OR TOD ACCOUNTS

Payable-on-death (POD) for bank accounts and transfer-on-death (TOD) for brokerage accounts (and, in some states, cars and houses) let an asset go straight to a named person at death, skipping probate completely. The named beneficiary just shows a death certificate and ID. No court order, no executor signature.

Other Real Estate

If there's a second home, rental property, land, or a cabin, each one needs to be inventoried, secured, and kept going. For rentals, that means continuing to collect rent (deposit into the estate account once it exists), handling tenants, keeping the place maintained. For land, paying property taxes and HOA dues. For vacation property, winterizing if needed.

If you can't manage a far-away property yourself, hire a property manager. The cost comes out of the estate, and the alternative — letting it degrade — costs way more.

Businesses

If the deceased owned a business, a piece of a business, or a professional practice, things get complicated fast. Short version:

- If there's a buy-sell agreement among the owners, find it. It usually spells out what happens when an owner dies — often a forced sale of the dead owner's share at a pre-agreed price.
- If there's no buy-sell, the business interest goes through the estate to whoever inherits it under the will (or under intestate rules). You hold the deceased's voting and management rights until distribution.
- Get a business attorney and a CPA who works with closely-held businesses. This is not a DIY category.

Chapter 8 covers when to bring in specialized help.

Personal Property

Jewelry, art, collectibles, silver, firearms, keepsakes. Three things to do:

1. **Inventory it.** Photograph each significant item. Estimate value or write "appraisal needed" if you don't know. Keep the list in the estate folder.
2. **Secure it.** High-value portable things — jewelry, watches, cash, small art — go into a safe deposit box, a home safe, or pro storage. Firearms have their own rules; some states require them turned over to a licensed dealer until the estate identifies a legal recipient.
3. **Don't distribute it yet.** Beneficiaries will ask for specific items immediately. The answer stays consistent: "After the estate is opened and we know what the will provides, we'll work through who gets what. Until then, everything is being held."

Digital Stuff

More and more of the estate lives online. Handle carefully:

- **Email accounts** — Gmail, Outlook, Apple. Don't log in even if you have the password. Most providers' terms of service ban third-party access, and some accounts auto-lock or wipe if accessed weirdly. Contact each provider's deceased-user team and follow their process.

- **Photo and document storage** — Google Drive, iCloud, Dropbox. Same. Family photos are often the most emotionally precious thing in the estate. Don't destroy them by triggering an account lockout.
- **Cryptocurrency** — find the wallet keys or recovery phrases. This is one place where lost keys means the asset is permanently gone. Search physical and digital storage thoroughly.
- **Subscriptions** — Netflix, Spotify, Amazon Prime, software. Cancel eventually; not urgent week one.
- **Social media** — Facebook, Instagram, LinkedIn. Most platforms have a "memorial" status. Wait until after the funeral.

> **KEY POINT**
>
> DO THIS NOW — Make one inventory sheet titled "Assets Secured." Rows: each asset (house, car, brokerage account, jewelry, etc.). Columns: where it is, rough value, what you did to secure it, the date. This sheet becomes the seed of the formal inventory you file with the court.

What This Looks Like in Practice

Two weeks after her uncle died, Sarah got a call from her uncle's neighbor. Someone had been seen walking out of the empty house with what looked like a painting.

Sarah had locked the front door but not changed the locks. She had not yet installed a keypad system. She had not asked the neighbors to keep an eye on the place.

When she got to the house, she found three pieces of furniture missing and an empty space on the wall where a framed lithograph had hung. She had photographed the lithograph the week before — wide shot, then close-up. The value, per a quick check of the artist online, was about $2,400.

Sarah filed a police report with the photographs attached. The lithograph was recovered three weeks later from a consignment shop two towns over. Sarah's photographs were the evidence that recovered it.

She also changed the locks that same afternoon, installed a keypad, asked the closest neighbor to check on the house daily, and adjusted her inventory log to mark the recovered piece. The other two pieces of furniture — value about $800 — were never recovered. She wrote the loss into the inventory and moved on.

What This Chapter Has Said

Notes from Real Estates

The first two weeks are when assets walk. Not usually because of bad intent — usually because of ambiguity. A cousin who genuinely thinks Mom "would have wanted me to have" the silver candlesticks. A neighbor who's been borrowing the lawnmower for ten years and now feels awkward about returning it.

A friend who took "just one painting" as a memento.

The cure is the photographs. You took them the first 72 hours. They're not for catching thieves. They're for preventing the awkward conversation where someone says they took something "with Mom's permission." The photographs make that conversation unnecessary.

Vehicles deserve more attention than most executors give them. A car parked on the street in front of an empty house gets noticed. Move it to the garage, the driveway, or off-site storage. Keep it insured.

Don't drive it for personal errands — the moment it's in an accident or stolen while in your custody, the question of personal liability gets complicated.

Patterns That Repeat

Pattern: the assumed-joint account that wasn't

A surviving spouse will often assume a particular account was held jointly with the deceased — and discover it wasn't. The account was solely in the deceased's name. It now belongs to the estate, not to the spouse.

Verify ownership of every account before you assume anything. Bank signature cards, brokerage account applications, and the deeds and titles on file at the county will tell you who actually owned what. Don't rely on what people remember; rely on what the documents say.

Pattern: the safety-deposit box no one can open

If the deceased had a safety-deposit box and you don't have the key — or you have the key but the bank won't let you in alone — most states have a specific procedure. Call the bank. Ask for the deceased-account team.

They can usually arrange a "will retrieval" opening (witnessed, with the bank's representative present, to remove the will only) or a full opening with court authorization.

Don't drill the box. Don't force it. The bank's procedure is faster and cheaper than what you'd otherwise do.

Pattern: the title that was never updated

A car, boat, or piece of land is titled to a parent who died years before the decedent. The deed never got re-recorded. Now you have two estates open at the same time — the one you are running, and a stale one that was never closed.

This is more common than people think. Pull every title and every deed for property you find. If the chain of title skips a step, call a probate attorney for the county where the property sits. Most states have a streamlined ancillary or summary procedure for this exact situation.

Pattern: the digital wallet nobody mentioned

Cryptocurrency, online brokerage cash, and prepaid debit cards routinely escape the first inventory pass because no paper statement arrives. Check the deceased's email for platform names — Coinbase, Robinhood, Cash App, PayPal — and check phone apps. If a balance exists, document it the day you find it; values move.

Figure 4.1

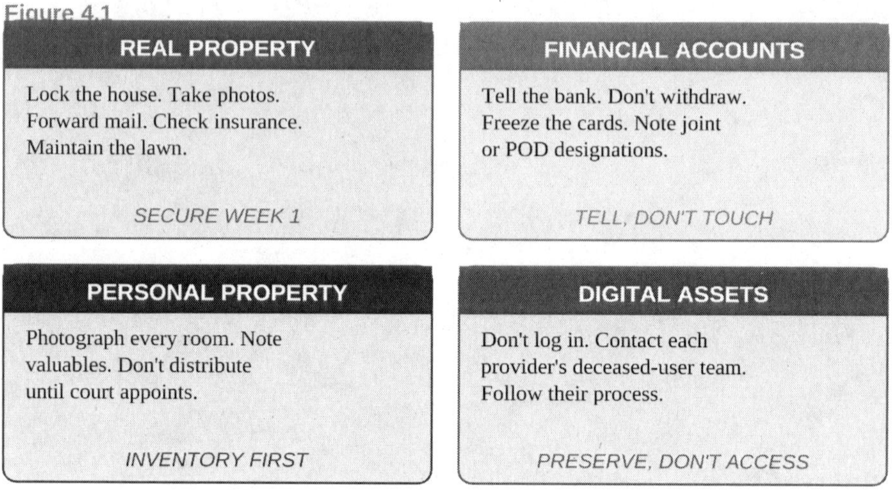

Four categories of assets to lock down in the first two weeks — real, financial, personal, digital.

If you cannot access a wallet because you do not have the private key or seed phrase, write that down too. The estate may still own the asset on paper; the practical recoverability is a separate question for the court.

Locking down assets is the first real operational job. The house gets locked, the mail forwarded, the neighbors told. Vehicles get insured and parked. Bank accounts get left alone but noted. Other real estate keeps running. Businesses get specialists. Personal property gets inventoried and held. Digital assets get preserved without logging in.

By the end of week two, every asset should be on the inventory sheet.

CHAPTER 5

Notifying Banks, Agencies, and Beneficiaries

Chapter at a Glance

- Who to notify in week 1, week 2, and weeks 3–4.
- Why the order matters (and which calls cut off identity theft).
- A sample letter you can send beneficiaries in the first month.
- The four questions beneficiaries will ask — and the right answers.
- What not to say in the first 60 days.

A death triggers a cascade of notifications. Some have to happen fast. Others can wait. A few you should deliberately put off. This chapter sorts them by urgency and audience, and gives you the basic language for each.

Two ground rules first:

- **Death certificates before anything else.** Most notifications require a certified copy. Order at least eight to ten in the first week through the funeral home or the state vital-records office. Each bank will want one and most won't give it back.

- **Written, not phoned in.** Almost every notification should be in writing, with proof you sent it. Email works for many. Certified mail for the ones where proof of delivery matters.

> **KEY POINT**
>
> Order matters. Tell Social Security before announcing the death publicly — identity thieves watch obituaries and open accounts within days. Tell the credit bureaus early. Put off some calls (employer benefits, life insurance) until you have the certified death certificate in hand, because they're all going to want it.

Week 1 — The Critical Calls

1. **Social Security.** If they were getting benefits, the funeral home usually files the death report electronically. Confirm it was filed. SSA will pull back any payment for the month of death and after. Spouses and dependents may qualify for survivor benefits — call 1-800-772-1213 to start.

2. **Pension plans**, if there was a pension. Call the administrator, identify yourself, ask them to stop payments and send any survivor-benefit forms.

3. **The employer**, if they were still working. HR needs to stop payroll, settle final wages, transition health benefits, and start the life-insurance or 401(k) process. Ask for a

contact and request, in writing, a summary of any death benefits, vacation owed, and deadlines.

4. **Credit bureaus** — Experian, Equifax, TransUnion. Send each a written notification with a death-certificate copy. This freezes new credit in the deceased's name. The bureaus mark the file as "deceased — do not issue credit."

5. **IRS Form 56** — once you're appointed, file this to put the IRS on notice that you're handling the deceased's tax stuff going forward.

Week 2 — Banks and Brokerages

1. **Each bank** holding an account. Walk in or call. Ask for the deceased-account specialist. They'll freeze new transactions, take the death certificate, and tell you what they need next (usually: certified letters of appointment, which you'll get from the court once you're officially in).

2. **Each brokerage and retirement custodian.** Same drill. Retirement accounts with named beneficiaries usually skip the estate entirely — but the custodian still needs to know about the death.

3. **Life insurance carriers** — each policy. The claim form is on the carrier's website. Simple claims are often paid in 10–14 days.

4. **Home, auto, and other property insurers.** Notify, don't cancel. Convert auto insurance to a non-driving or

storage policy on cars being held.

5. **Mortgage company.** Just tell them. Mortgages usually keep going for inherited family homes without trouble, but they need to know where to send the statements.

6. **Utilities.** Keep service active. Don't transfer accounts into your name yet. Pay bills from the estate account once it's open.

Week 3 to Week 4 — The Beneficiaries

Beneficiaries are entitled to know the death happened and that they're named in the will. They're not entitled to a copy of the will until it's been filed with the court (at which point it's public anyway). They're not entitled to a distribution until creditors are paid and the court has signed off.

A simple letter to each beneficiary in the first 30 days does the job. Something like this:

FIRST LETTER TO A BENEFICIARY

"Dear [Name], As you may know, [Deceased] passed away on [date]. I've been named in their will as executor. You're named as a beneficiary. I'm in the process of filing the will with the [County] Probate Court and asking to be formally appointed. Once the court appoints me and admits the will, you'll get a copy of the will and a notice of your specific interest. Estate administration usually takes nine to fifteen months. I'll send periodic updates and a final accounting before any distribution. Please send me your current mailing address so I can keep you in the loop. With appreciation, [Your name]."

Send it certified mail with return receipt, and keep the receipts. The letter does three things at once: it satisfies your duty to tell them, it sets realistic time expectations (heading off the "why is this taking so long" calls), and it creates a paper trail showing you communicated in good faith.

What Not to Say in the First 60 Days

Beneficiaries will ask specific questions. Defer most of them.

- **"How much am I getting?"** Answer: "The estate is being inventoried and the will should be admitted in [month]. I'll have a clearer picture in 90 days. Until then, I don't have a reliable number."
- **"When will I get it?"** Answer: "After creditors are handled, taxes are filed, and the court signs off. Usually nine to fifteen months."
- **"Can I have [item] now?"** Answer: "All personal property is being held by the estate until distribution. Make a list of items you're particularly interested in and send it to me, and I'll factor it in when we get there."
- **"Did Dad really leave it all to her?"** Answer: "The will is being filed and will be public once admitted. I'd rather not characterize what it says before then."

These aren't dodges. They're the right answers. They're also what keeps a beneficiary from later claiming you misled them. Be warm. Be patient. Defer.

What This Looks Like in Practice

Mike sent his beneficiary-notification letter on March 15, thirty-two days after his father's death. Six people got the letter — his three siblings, his stepmother, a niece, and the local hospital foundation (which was named for a modest specific bequest).

His stepmother called within an hour. "What's the timeline? When will I get my share? Is the will being changed?"

Mike answered the same way he was going to answer for the next eleven months: "The will is being filed with the probate court. Estate administration usually takes nine to fifteen months. I'll send a monthly update, and you'll get a final accounting before any distribution.

The will is the will — I don't have authority to change it, and I wouldn't want to."

His stepmother was disappointed by the lack of detail. She was also visibly relieved by the calm. Two of Mike's siblings later told him the same letter had landed for them — warm, informative, with no manufactured drama. The estate closed in eleven months. Mike sent a final brief thank-you note when it was over.

Two of the recipients wrote back to thank him.

What This Chapter Has Said

Notes from Real Estates

The monthly update letter is the best executor tool nobody talks about. Two paragraphs. Same day each month. Same template every time. Status of major tasks. Expected next steps. Expected closing date.

Beneficiaries who get these letters call you less. They fight less. They sign their releases faster. They thank you more often. The letters take fifteen minutes to write each month and they save you hours of one-off phone calls and weeks of trust-building you'd otherwise have to do during the closing phase.

The phrase "the will says what it says" is your friend. Beneficiaries will ask for explanations, exceptions, modifications, side deals. Each time, the right answer is some version of: "The will says what it says. I don't have authority to change it, and I wouldn't want to." Say it warmly. Mean it. Then move on.

Patterns That Repeat

Pattern: the obituary that triggers identity theft

Obituaries are public. They contain a name, an approximate date of birth, a place of residence, and often the names of immediate family members. That's almost everything an identity thief needs to open an account.

Notify the three credit bureaus before the obituary runs. Each will flag the file as deceased within a couple of days, and credit-application attempts after that will fail automatically. Without this step, you may spend months disputing fraudulent accounts. With it, the obituary becomes safe to publish.

Pattern: the Social Security overpayment

Social Security pays benefits monthly, by direct deposit, for the month of receipt. If a beneficiary dies on the 5th of the month, the payment for that month was made on the 3rd — before the death. SSA will recall that payment.

Don't spend it. Don't transfer it. If the account it was deposited into is going to be closed, contact the bank and arrange for the recall payment to be honored even after closing. SSA handles this every day; the procedure is routine.

Pattern: the well-meaning friend who tells everyone

A neighbor or close friend hears the news, then calls every subscription and service the deceased had to "help out." They mean well. The result is a stack of refund-pending items, missed automatic charges, and businesses asking for death certificates you have not yet ordered.

Ask the family to route every account-related call through you. Make a single page in your notebook listing what the friend already cancelled, and follow up to confirm the refund actually arrived. The work is now yours either way; the goal is to know what was touched.

Pattern: the pension that keeps paying

Figure 5.1

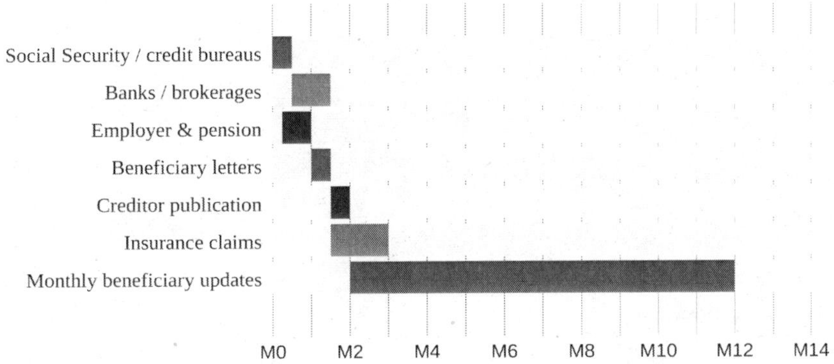

The notification cascade — who gets told when, from week one through month twelve.

Defined-benefit pensions and some employer survivor benefits continue paying for one or two cycles after death. The estate is usually obligated to return the over-payment. The pension administrator will send a letter; do not ignore it.

Open a single folder marked "recovery" for over-payments — Social Security, pensions, the last automatic refund from the insurer — and log every item. When the estate closes, the recovery folder is the proof you did not pocket money that did not belong to the estate.

Notifications follow a sequence: agencies and credit bureaus first, banks and brokerages next, beneficiaries by the end of the first month. Each in writing. Each backed up by a death certificate. The order matters because it cuts off identity theft and sets the cadence of the estate. Beneficiary questions get warm, patient, accurate deferrals — not speculation.

CHAPTER 6

Handling Debts and Outstanding Obligations

Chapter at a Glance

- How the creditor-claim process actually works.
- The order debts get paid when there isn't enough to pay everyone.
- Specific guidance for credit cards, mortgages, medical, student loans, and taxes.
- What an insolvent estate looks like — and what it does not push onto family.
- Why paying too early throws away your leverage.

The deceased almost certainly owed money to someone. Credit cards, a mortgage, a car loan, medical bills, maybe student loans, maybe back taxes. The estate handles them. Beneficiaries don't — with a handful of specific exceptions.

This chapter walks through what gets paid, in what order, from what money, and what happens when the estate doesn't have enough to pay everything.

> **KEY POINT**
>
> Beneficiaries do not inherit debts. They inherit what's left after debts are paid. If the debts are bigger than the assets, the beneficiaries get nothing — but they don't write checks from their own pocket. The main exception: co-signed debt. A co-signer stays on the hook personally.

How the Creditor Process Works

Most states ask you to do two things to give creditors a fair shot:

1. **Publish a notice** in a local newspaper. It's a small classified ad: "The estate of [Deceased] is in administration; creditors must present claims within [period]." The court has a template. It runs $40–$150.
2. **Send direct written notice** to creditors you can identify. These are the ones whose names show up in the deceased's records — the credit-card companies on the statements, the mortgage company, the medical providers who've billed.

After publication and notice, creditors have a window — usually four to six months, depending on the state — to present claims. Anything they don't present in that window is barred forever. This is one of the few mechanisms that protects the estate from being haunted by old debts you never knew about.

The Order Money Gets Paid

When there are several creditors and the estate has limited money, the law says who gets paid first. The exact order varies slightly by state, but the typical priority is:

1. Costs of running the estate — court fees, attorney fees, executor fees, accountant fees, the newspaper notice. These come off the top.

2. Funeral and burial costs, up to a reasonable amount.

3. Last-illness medical expenses.

4. Federal taxes (income tax for the year of death, plus estate tax if the estate is big enough — which most aren't).

5. State taxes.

6. Secured debts — mortgages, car loans. These get paid out of what the collateral is worth; any shortfall drops to the unsecured pile.

7. Unsecured debts — credit cards, personal loans, unsecured medical bills, court judgments. These get paid out of what's left, often pro-rata when there isn't enough.

8. Beneficiary distributions — dead last. They happen only after everything above has been handled.

AN INSOLVENT ESTATE

An estate is "insolvent" when the debts are bigger than the assets. The executor pays the legally required priorities (estate costs, funeral, taxes, secured debts) out of whatever's available, and the lower-priority creditors and the beneficiaries get nothing. Insolvent estates do not push debt onto family members — unless those family members co-signed or were jointly liable. Your job in an insolvent estate is to handle the priorities in order and close the file.

The Specific Categories

Credit cards. Tell each issuer in writing with a death certificate. Close the card. Don't pay until they present a claim through the formal process. If you (or anyone) co-signed or jointly held the card, that person stays on the hook for charges through the date of death.

Mortgages. The mortgage keeps running. The estate pays the monthly amount until the house is sold or transferred. If a beneficiary inherits the house, they either take over the mortgage, refinance, or sell. Federal law generally protects family transfers from triggering a "pay-it-all-now" clause, but read the loan docs.

Car loans. Same. The estate pays until the car is sold or transferred. If nobody wants the car and the estate is selling it, pay the loan off from the sale. If the car is worth less than the loan, the lender either takes it back (and the shortfall is a normal unsecured claim) or accepts surrender.

Medical debt. Tell each provider. A lot of bills that arrive after death turn out to be partially or fully covered by Medicare, Medicaid, or supplemental insurance once death is processed. Wait 60–90 days before paying anything — the bills almost always shrink.

Federal student loans get discharged at death. Tell the loan servicer with a death certificate. Private student loans often survive death and become claims against the estate. Check each loan's specific terms.

Tax debts. The estate is responsible for the deceased's final income-tax return (the one for the year they died, due April 15 of the year after), any tax returns for the estate itself during administration, and a special estate-tax return if the estate is in the millions of dollars (most aren't). You sign these as executor.

Get a CPA who's done estate work before.

What Beneficiaries Are Not on the Hook For

Worth repeating, because it comes up constantly:

- Beneficiaries are not personally responsible for the deceased's unsecured debts.
- Beneficiaries are not personally responsible for credit-card debt unless they co-signed or were jointly named.

• Beneficiaries are not personally responsible for medical debt.

• Beneficiaries are not personally responsible for tax debts.

• Beneficiaries are personally responsible only for debt they themselves co-signed — a joint mortgage, a co-signed business loan, a joint car loan.

When a creditor calls a beneficiary directly demanding payment, the right answer is: "The estate is being handled by [executor name]. Send your claim in writing to [executor address] within the statutory window. I'm not personally responsible for this debt."

Keep a Log

For every debt you handle, write down:

1. Creditor name and contact.
2. Date the original debt was incurred.
3. Amount claimed.
4. Date you got the claim or notice.
5. Date and amount of any payment.
6. Where the money came from (estate account, sale proceeds, etc.).
7. Final outcome (paid, partially settled, denied, time-barred).

The log becomes part of your final accounting to the court. It's also your defense if a creditor later says they weren't paid: documented good-faith handling is the executor's protection.

> **KEY POINT**
>
> DO THIS NOW — Before paying any credit card, medical bill, or unsecured debt, wait for the creditor to present a formal claim in writing. Many will get reduced or wiped out by insurance, by the statutory deadline, or by negotiation. Paying early throws away your leverage.

What This Looks Like in Practice

Donna's mother had $42,000 in credit-card debt across four cards when she died. The estate had about $80,000 in assets after the funeral and administration costs were paid.

Donna did not pay any of the credit-card balances immediately. She published the creditor notice, sent direct written notice to each card issuer, and waited.

Over the next four months, three of the four card issuers presented formal claims. The fourth never did — that balance, about $7,200, was barred when the creditor-claim window closed.

Of the three that did present claims, two negotiated down (one to 70% of the balance, one to 50% in exchange for immediate payment), and the third was paid in full at $18,000.

By the end, Donna had paid approximately $28,000 against what had originally been $42,000 in claimed debt. The remaining $14,000 in nominal balance was either negotiated away or barred. The two beneficiaries — Donna and her brother — received about $26,000 each from the remaining estate.

Had Donna paid the full $42,000 within the first month, each would have received about $19,000 instead. The patience was worth $14,000.

What This Chapter Has Said

Notes from Real Estates

Medical bills almost always shrink. Bills that arrive in the first month after death are usually the gross amount, before Medicare, Medicaid, and supplemental insurance reconciliation. Wait 60–90 days. The bill you got for $14,000 often becomes a bill for $1,800 once insurance catches up. Pay nothing immediately.

Credit-card claims are often dropped if not promptly presented. Card issuers know that estate-claim presentation requires paperwork — a written notice within the statutory window. About a third of the time, especially with smaller balances, they don't bother. The balance becomes time-barred.

You can verify this in your final accounting by noting which creditors were notified and which actually presented claims. Don't volunteer payment for balances that haven't been formally claimed.

The IRS is patient but not forgetful. Tax debts owed by the deceased survive death and become claims against the estate. The IRS will work with you on timing. They will not work with you on whether the obligation exists. If your CPA finds an unfiled return or an unpaid balance, deal with it directly.

Don't let it linger; interest and penalties keep growing.

Patterns That Repeat

Pattern: the creditor who doesn't claim

A credit-card company carries a $4,000 balance. You send them written notice of the death within 30 days. The statutory creditor-claim window in your state is six months. The card issuer never presents a formal written claim within the window.

After the window closes, the debt is barred. You do not pay it. You document, in the final accounting, that the notice was sent (with proof of delivery) and that no formal claim was received within the statutory period. The estate moves on.

This isn't sleazy. The creditor had a fair opportunity and chose not to exercise it. The statutory framework exists precisely to put a stake in the ground so estates can close.

Pattern: the medical bill that turns into a refund

A hospital bill arrives for $24,000 for the deceased's final week of care. You wait. Sixty days later, the bill is reissued at $2,800 after Medicare and supplemental insurance have reconciled. Ninety days later, after Medicaid recovery is applied, the bill is $0 — and a $400 refund check arrives for the unused portion of the deceased's last copay.

Figure 6.1

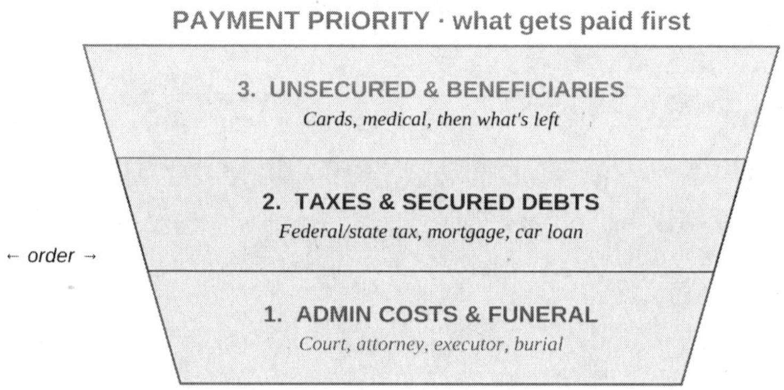

Payment priority — who gets paid first when the estate has limited money.

Had you paid the $24,000 immediately, you'd have spent months trying to claw back the overpayment from a hospital billing department. By waiting, you let the billing reconcile and the right number emerge on its own. Patience pays — sometimes literally.

The estate handles debts. Beneficiaries don't. Notice goes out in the newspaper and to known creditors directly. Creditors have a limited window. Payment follows a priority order. Different kinds of debt — cards, mortgages, medical, student loans, taxes — have different practical rules. Beneficiaries are personally on the hook only for debt they themselves co-signed. Document everything.

Don't pay too early.

PART 3

◆

APPLICATION

Now you do the work — managing the assets day to day, knowing when to bring in a lawyer, and getting everything to the right person at the end.

CHAPTER 7

Managing Property, Accounts, and Valuables

Chapter at a Glance

- How to open the estate's own bank account (and why this matters).
- Getting the EIN — ten minutes, free, at IRS.gov.
- How to track every dollar without losing your mind.
- What to do with the real estate, the investments, and the business.
- A structured process for distributing personal property without family fights.

Probate is not instant. The estate exists as a working entity for months — sometimes more than a year. During that time, things have to keep running. Bills have to get paid. The house needs the lawn mowed. Investments need someone watching them. Tenants need a landlord. Property taxes don't pause because someone died.

This chapter is about the day-to-day of running the estate. It starts with the one thing you have to set up before you can do anything else: the estate's own bank account.

> **KEY POINT**
>
> The estate is its own thing. It has its own bank account, its own tax ID number, its own records. Money goes into it. Money goes out of it. None of it touches your personal money. Get this wrong and everything else gets complicated.

Step One: Open the Estate Account

Once the court appoints you (you'll get a document called Letters Testamentary or Letters of Administration — same idea, different name), you can open a bank account in the estate's name. Here's what you need to bring:

1. **Certified death certificate** (the bank keeps one).
2. **Your Letters Testamentary** (proof from the court that you're the executor).
3. **An EIN for the estate** — this is the tax ID number for the estate, separate from the deceased's Social Security number. You get one for free in about ten minutes online at IRS.gov. Search "apply for EIN."
4. **Your own ID.**
5. **Some money to deposit** — even $25 is fine. You can fund it later from the deceased's other accounts.

Pick a checking account, not a savings account. You'll need to write checks. Pick a bank that already had a relationship with the deceased if possible — moving money inside the same bank is faster than wiring it across institutions. Get a debit card tied to the account only if you must; the paper trail is cleaner without one.

Online banking, on the other hand, is your friend.

From this point on, every dollar that touches the estate goes through this account. Sale proceeds. Refunds. Insurance payouts. All deposits. Every payment — to the funeral home, to creditors, to tax authorities, to the attorney — gets written from this account. No exceptions.

Not "I'll reimburse myself later." Not "I'll just put it on my credit card and pay myself back."

Tracking the Money

You're going to be asked, at the end, for a complete accounting of every dollar in and every dollar out. Most courts have a specific form. The form is straightforward — it's basically a checkbook register — but if you haven't been keeping records, reconstructing months of transactions later is a nightmare.

Build the habit from day one:

- Use a spreadsheet, accounting software, or just a paper ledger.
- Log every transaction the same day or the same week.
- For every outgoing payment, note (a) what it was for, (b) who got it, (c) the date, (d) the check number or transaction

reference.

- For every incoming payment, note (a) the source, (b) the amount, (c) the date.
- Keep paper receipts for everything in a single envelope or folder. You don't have to organize them perfectly; you just need them to exist.

Done weekly, this is maybe ten minutes. Skipped for two months, it's a Saturday of misery.

Real Estate During Administration

If the estate includes a house — and it usually does — keep it maintained. Specifically:

- **Pay the mortgage** out of the estate account each month, on time. Late fees are stupid, avoidable expenses.
- **Pay property taxes** when they come due. Unpaid property taxes can lead to tax liens, which are painful to clear up.
- **Keep the insurance current.** Many home insurance policies have a clause saying coverage drops or ends if the home is vacant for 30+ days. Call the carrier, tell them the situation, and either keep the policy active under a "vacant home" rider or switch to a vacant-home policy. Don't just let it lapse.
- **Keep up the basic maintenance.** Lawn mowed, gutters clear, leaves raked. The neighbors will appreciate it and

you'll get more for the place when you sell.

- **Winterize if it's empty.** In cold climates, that means setting the heat above freezing, having a plumber drain pipes if you're closing the house up, and checking on the property periodically.
- **Document the condition** with photos every couple of months. A vacant house can be vandalized, broken into, or damaged by weather. You want pictures of what it looked like throughout.

Investments During Administration

Brokerage accounts, retirement accounts, and any other investments need supervision. The default rule is: don't move things around. Don't make big trades. Don't try to time the market. The estate is going to distribute these assets soon anyway, and your job during administration is preservation, not maximization.

Specifically:

- **Don't sell stocks just because the market is volatile.** Volatility is normal. Your job is to get the assets safely to the beneficiaries, not to outperform an index.
- **Do collect dividends and interest** into the estate account. Most brokerage accounts can be set to automatic deposit.

- **Do reinvest dividends if the deceased had that set up** — unless you're planning to sell the position soon, in which case let dividends drop to cash.
- **Don't transfer retirement accounts into the estate.** IRAs and 401(k)s with named beneficiaries skip the estate entirely. Those beneficiaries claim directly from the custodian. The estate's job is to identify the accounts and notify the custodian; the custodian handles the rest.
- **Do consider hiring a fee-only financial advisor** if the estate has substantial investment assets and you're not comfortable making decisions. The estate pays. A flat-fee, hourly advisor is usually cheaper than a percentage-based advisor for the short engagement an estate needs.

Selling Assets During Administration

Some assets have to be sold during administration — either because nobody wants them, or because the estate needs cash to pay debts, or because the will directs a sale.

A few rules:

- **Get a real valuation.** For real estate, that means a licensed appraisal (typically $400–$800). For collectibles, jewelry, art, antiques — a written appraisal from a qualified appraiser. For vehicles, a written quote from a dealer plus a check of the Kelley Blue Book or NADA value.

- **Sell at arm's length.** Don't sell to yourself. Don't sell to your spouse. Don't sell to a beneficiary for less than the appraised value without all the beneficiaries agreeing in writing — and even then, run it past the lawyer.
- **Document the offering process.** If you sold the house, what did you list it for? Who saw it? What were the offers? Take screenshots. Save the listing photos. The accounting will ask.
- **Use the estate account.** Sale proceeds go in. Selling expenses (real estate commission, repair costs, listing fees) come out. Net proceeds stay in the account until distribution.

Personal Property: Who Gets What

This is the category families fight over most. Not because it's the most valuable — usually it isn't — but because objects carry memories, and memories don't divide evenly.

A structured approach saves a lot of grief. Here's one that works:

1. **Inventory the personal property.** Photograph each item or group. Estimate values.
2. **Identify items the will specifically gives to specific people.** Those are easy — set them aside, marked.
3. **For everything else, propose a process** to the beneficiaries: a rotating draft (eldest first, then youngest,

then next eldest, etc.), or an auction-style "bid points" system (each beneficiary gets, say, 100 points and bids), or a simple round-robin.

4. **Get everyone's agreement in writing** before you start. "I, [Beneficiary], agree to the distribution method [described] for the personal property of [Deceased]."
5. **Run the process.** Document the outcome.
6. **Have each beneficiary sign a receipt** for what they took.

The structure prevents the fight. The fight isn't really about the silverware. It's about being heard and being fair. A transparent process — agreed in advance, run consistently — handles both.

> **KEY POINT**
>
> DO THIS NOW — Open the estate bank account this week if you haven't already. Apply for the EIN online (10 minutes, free). Get the Letters Testamentary from the court (they're issued at your appointment hearing). Walk into the bank with the death certificate, the Letters, the EIN, and your ID. From this point on, every dollar runs through that account.

What This Looks Like in Practice

Tom opened the estate bank account at his father's bank — the same bank his father had used for forty years — on the Wednesday after his appointment hearing. He brought a certified death certificate, his Letters Testamentary, the EIN confirmation he'd printed off IRS.gov that morning, his driver's license, and $50 in cash.

The bank's deceased-account specialist handled the whole thing in about forty minutes. The new account had Tom's name on it as executor, the estate's EIN, online banking access, and a single ATM card Tom asked to be issued but never used. From that morning forward, every dollar that moved through the estate moved through that account.

Six months later, when a beneficiary called to ask why a particular invoice had been paid, Tom pulled up the transaction in online banking, screenshotted it, and emailed it within fifteen minutes. The question went away. So did three or four others over the following months.

The estate account was the answer to every "where did the money go" question — and it was the answer every time, because every dollar had been logged.

What This Chapter Has Said

Notes from Real Estates

The estate account is where the audit trail lives. Every dollar that comes in or goes out leaves a record. Six months later, when a beneficiary asks why a particular check was written, you pull up online banking, screenshot the transaction, and email it within minutes.

Without the estate account, that same answer requires reconstructing your personal bank statements, separating estate transactions from your own, and producing a narrative you can't easily back up.

Real estate during administration is where surprise expenses live. The HVAC fails. The roof leaks. The water heater goes. The tree falls. Budget for surprises. Keep $5,000–$10,000 of the estate account liquid for property maintenance. Better to have it and not need it than to scramble when something breaks.

Personal-property distribution is where the family wounds appear. A structured process — agreed in writing, run consistently, documented carefully — is the difference between estate closures with hugs at the end and ones with lawyers at the end. It's almost never about the value of the items. It's about being heard. The structure is how you make sure everyone is.

Patterns That Repeat

Pattern: the brokerage that requires "Medallion Signature Guarantee"

When you transfer securities from the deceased's brokerage account to the estate account — or eventually to the beneficiaries — the brokerage will often require a Medallion Signature Guarantee. This is a specific kind of authentication, more rigorous than a notary, performed by a bank or brokerage that participates in the program.

Two things to know. First: not every bank does Medallions. Call ahead. Your local credit union may not. Larger national banks usually do. Second: many brokerages will issue the guarantee themselves if you're transferring to an account at the same firm. The brokerage doing the transfer is often the easiest path.

Pattern: the rental property that needs an interim manager

If the estate includes a rental property, someone has to be the landlord during administration. Collecting rent. Handling tenant issues. Coordinating repairs. This is either you, a co-executor, or a hired property manager.

Hiring a property manager runs 8–12% of monthly rent. Worth it if the property is more than an hour's drive from where you live, if the tenant has complex needs, or if there are multiple units. The expense is reimbursable from the estate.

The alternative — managing it yourself from a distance — usually costs more in time and in missed maintenance than the management fee saves.

Pattern: the appraisal that surprises the family

Date-of-death valuations sometimes come in well below what the family thought the asset was worth. A house Mom told everyone was "worth at least four hundred thousand" appraises at three-twenty. A coin collection a sibling remembers as priceless turns out to be worth four thousand. The appraiser is rarely wrong; family memory is rarely accurate.

Walk the family through the appraisal report before any distribution conversation. Show the comparable sales for real estate; show the auction-house guides for personal property. The number on the report is what the IRS and the court will accept. The number anyone remembered is not.

Pattern: the closely-held business with no buy-sell

If the deceased owned all or part of a small business — an S-corp, an LLC, a partnership — and there is no written buy-sell agreement, the estate now owns that interest with no automatic path to exit.

Figure 7.1

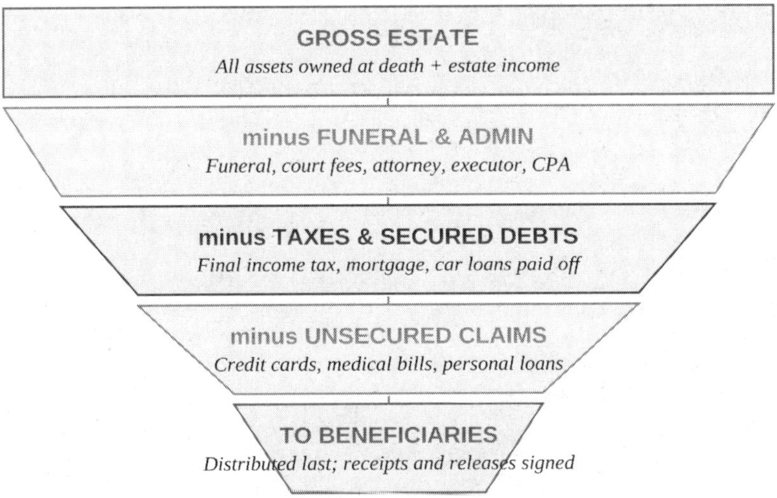

How estate money flows — from gross estate to beneficiaries, with debts and taxes in between.

The surviving partners may want to buy out the estate, but they will quote a number that serves them; the estate may want to sell, but it has no ready market.

Get a third-party business valuation before any negotiation. The valuation costs $3,000 to $10,000 and establishes a defensible number for the estate's books and for any beneficiary who later asks how the price was set. Do not let a co-owner draft both sides of the deal.

Running the estate means keeping the lights on for nine to fifteen months. Open the estate bank account first. Track every dollar in and out. Maintain the real estate. Don't gamble with the investments. Sell assets at fair value through documented processes. Use a structured method for personal property, agreed by everyone in writing. Then it gets distributed.

CHAPTER 8

Working with Attorneys (When and When Not To)

Chapter at a Glance

- When you genuinely need a lawyer (eight situations).
- When you probably don't (and can save the estate thousands).
- The three questions to ask any attorney before you hire.
- How probate attorneys bill — and what's fair.
- How to manage the relationship so the lawyer works for you.

Most executors hire a lawyer. Most don't need one for everything. Knowing where the line is can save the estate thousands of dollars and save you weeks of waiting on a return phone call.

This chapter walks through when a lawyer is genuinely needed, when you can handle something yourself, how to choose one if you need one, what they should and shouldn't charge for, and how to stay in control of the relationship.

> **KEY POINT**
>
> A probate lawyer is a specialist you hire for specific tasks, not a manager who runs the estate. You are the executor. The lawyer works for the estate, through you. If your lawyer is making decisions you don't understand, that's a problem to fix — not a feature to accept.

When You Genuinely Need a Lawyer

These are the situations where you should hire one:

- **The will is being contested.** Someone is challenging the will's validity, claiming undue influence, fraud, or lack of capacity. You need a litigator immediately.
- **The estate is insolvent or close to it.** When creditors will be paid in priority order and some won't be paid at all, you need a lawyer to handle the math and the negotiations cleanly.
- **There's real estate in more than one state.** Probate happens in each state where the deceased owned real property. You'll need an attorney in each.
- **The estate has tax exposure.** Federal estate tax (rare) or a state estate tax (more common — about a dozen states have one with thresholds below the federal level) requires specialized return preparation.
- **There's a business interest.** Closely-held businesses, professional practices, family LLCs — all of these need both a probate attorney and probably a CPA who specializes in business succession.

- **Family conflict has surfaced.** Two beneficiaries are already arguing, threats of litigation have been made, or you're worried about being sued personally. A lawyer protects you.
- **The estate is large.** "Large" is relative, but generally over $1–2 million in assets — the complexity grows non-linearly above that line.
- **You're the executor but you're also a beneficiary in a way that creates potential conflict.** You inherit the family business; your siblings don't. You need an attorney to keep the conflict-of-interest charges off your record.

When You Probably Don't Need a Lawyer

For straightforward estates, you can often handle the whole thing with the court's self-help materials, a CPA for the tax returns, and a few specific consultations with an attorney billed by the hour. "Straightforward" usually means:

- The will is clear and uncontested.
- The estate is under $1 million in assets.
- All beneficiaries are getting along.
- Real estate is in one state and is being sold or passing cleanly to one person.
- There's no business interest.
- There's no federal or state estate tax exposure.
- Creditors will be paid in full with money to spare.

If most of those are true, you can often do this with a few hours of attorney time spent on specific questions, rather than hiring a lawyer to run the case.

Finding a Lawyer (If You Need One)

Three questions in order of importance:

1. **Do they specialize in probate?** Not estate planning (that's the work people do *before* they die). Probate is what happens *after*. Different specialty, different skills. Ask directly: "What percentage of your practice is probate administration?" You want at least 30%.
2. **Have they handled an estate like this one before?** A small clean estate? A contested will? A business succession? Ask for an example. The answer reveals the depth of their experience.
3. **How do they bill?** Flat fee for the whole administration? Hourly with a written estimate? Percentage of estate assets? You want to understand exactly what you're agreeing to.

Get two or three consultations before you hire. Most probate attorneys offer a free initial consultation of 30–60 minutes. Use it to ask the three questions above and to gauge how comfortable you feel with them. Trust matters a lot in this relationship — you're going to share the family's financial and emotional history.

How They Bill — And What's Fair

Probate attorneys typically bill one of three ways:

- **Flat fee** for the whole administration, often $2,500–$8,000 for a straightforward estate, more for complex ones. The advantage: predictability. The disadvantage: the lawyer's incentive is to do the minimum.
- **Hourly**, typically $200–$500/hour depending on the market. The advantage: you only pay for what you actually need. The disadvantage: the bill can balloon if you're not careful.
- **Percentage of estate assets**, typically 2–5%. Some states actually set statutory fees this way by default. The advantage: simple. The disadvantage: the fee can be wildly out of proportion to the work, especially for large estates with simple administration.

Whatever the billing structure, get the engagement in writing. The letter (sometimes called a "retainer agreement" or "engagement letter") should spell out: the scope of work, the fee structure, what's covered and what costs extra, how disputes get handled, and how to terminate the relationship.

What to Hire Them For — and What to Do Yourself

Hire the lawyer for:

- Preparing and filing the petition for probate.
- Representing you at any court hearings.

• Drafting and serving formal notices to beneficiaries and creditors.

• Handling any disputes — will contests, creditor objections, beneficiary disagreements that escalate.

• Preparing the final accounting and the petition to close the estate.

• Real-estate transfers (often a separate transactional attorney does this, but the probate attorney can usually coordinate).

Do yourself:

• Banking. Open the account, deposit money, write checks, reconcile statements.

• Inventory. Walk the house with a camera and a clipboard.

• Mail handling. Open it, sort it, log what matters.

• Day-to-day communication with beneficiaries. Letters, phone calls, scheduling.

• Maintaining the real estate.

• Cataloging personal property.

• Bookkeeping — tracking every dollar in and out.

The single biggest mistake executors make is having the lawyer do everything. Lawyers cost $300–$500 an hour. Photocopying shouldn't be billed at $400 an hour. Sorting through old statements shouldn't either. Keep the lawyer focused on the legal work and do the administrative work yourself.

Managing the Relationship

Some habits that keep the lawyer working for you:

- **Send written questions, not phone calls.** Email is your friend. It creates a record and forces specific answers.
- **Batch your questions.** Don't email five times a day. Save up the questions and send them once a week.
- **Ask for an estimate before any major task.** "Before you draft this, how many hours do you expect this to take?" The answer doesn't have to be precise; it just keeps everyone aligned.
- **Read every bill.** Not just the total. Read the line items. If something doesn't make sense, ask. Polite, specific questions about a bill are routine. Most lawyers respect the executor who reads the bill.
- **Don't be afraid to push back.** "That feels expensive — can you explain what was involved?" is a perfectly reasonable question. So is "Could we handle that in-house instead?"

When to Switch Lawyers

If your lawyer stops returning calls, misses court deadlines, or runs up bills you don't understand, you can fire them. The estate's documents are the estate's property; the lawyer must turn them over. The replacement lawyer can take over from where the first one left off.

It's painful, but it's a normal occurrence — don't be reluctant if the relationship has broken down.

What you usually shouldn't do is fire a lawyer mid-litigation. If you're in the middle of a will contest or a creditor dispute, finishing that piece with the existing lawyer is usually better than starting over. Switch after that fight is resolved, if you must.

> **KEY POINT**
>
> DO THIS NOW — Before your first attorney consultation, write down: (1) the size and rough complexity of the estate, (2) specific concerns you have (contests? out-of-state property? business?), (3) your three questions about specialization, experience, and billing. Walk into the consultation with this page. You will get a much better conversation.

What This Looks Like in Practice

Linda hired a probate attorney for $4,500 to handle her uncle's estate. The estate had about $600,000 in assets, no business interests, no real estate outside her state, and three uncontested beneficiaries.

Halfway through, she realized the attorney was billing for tasks she could have done herself — sorting mail, photocopying receipts, walking documents to the bank. Her monthly invoices were running $1,200 a month and growing.

Linda called the attorney's office and asked for a conversation. "I think I can take some of this off your plate. Can we agree that you'll handle the court filings and the legal questions, and I'll do the banking, the inventory work, and the beneficiary communication?"

The attorney agreed cheerfully. From that month on, the bills dropped to about $400 a month, mostly for filings and short legal questions. By the time the estate closed, Linda had saved approximately $5,000 by doing the administrative work herself — money that went to the beneficiaries instead of to the law firm. The attorney did not mind.

Most probate attorneys would prefer not to do clerical work at $400 an hour.

What This Chapter Has Said

Notes from Real Estates

Lawyers cost what they cost, but their incentive is to do the legal work, not the clerical work. Most experienced probate attorneys would prefer the executor handle the administrative side. They'd rather spend their billed hours on the petition, the accounting, the occasional dispute — the things that genuinely require legal training.

The clerical hours are a chore for them and an expense for you. The conversation "can we handle this in-house instead?" is one most lawyers welcome.

Get the engagement letter and read it. The two or three pages spell out exactly what's covered, how billing works, what counts as a separate matter (and so a separate bill), and how the relationship ends. Most disagreements with probate attorneys come from misunderstandings of the engagement letter, not from bad lawyering. Read it before you sign.

Ask questions about anything that isn't clear.

Switch if you must, but pick your moment. If the lawyer stops returning calls or runs up bills you can't justify, you can fire them. The replacement takes the files over and continues from where the first one left off. Avoid switching mid-litigation — finishing a will contest with the existing attorney is usually better than starting over.

Switch between phases, not in the middle of one.

Patterns That Repeat

Pattern: the attorney who quotes a flat fee but bills the estate as a percentage

Some attorneys quote you a flat fee for the engagement but, in the engagement letter, reserve the right to charge a percentage of estate assets if the estate is larger than expected. Read the letter carefully.

A flat $4,000 fee can become a $25,000 fee if the estate turns out to be $1 million. Negotiate the structure up front. Most attorneys will agree to a true flat fee, or to an hourly rate, if asked plainly. They reserve percentage billing for clients who don't ask. Ask.

Pattern: the attorney who hands work back to you anyway

Some attorneys, especially in smaller practices, will tell you they need you to gather all the documents, fill out the forms, and do the leg work — and then they'll review and file. This can be a great arrangement if it's reflected in the fee.

Verify in the engagement letter that you're paying for the legal review and filing work, not for clerical handling you're already doing yourself. The fee should match the actual work. If you're doing 80% of the work, the fee should reflect that you're doing 80% of the work.

Pattern: the second opinion that saves five figures

When an attorney quotes the engagement, ask for a written scope and a written estimate. Then take both to one other probate attorney in the same county for a thirty-minute consult. Most offer a free initial review. You are not shopping the case; you are pressure-testing the scope.

Figure 8.1

Three ways to handle the legal work — DIY, hourly attorney, or full-service representation.

Probate fees that look reasonable in the first meeting often turn out to be three to five times the local norm once a second attorney has seen the file. The second opinion sometimes confirms the first quote; sometimes it saves the estate ten or fifteen thousand dollars.

Either way, the estate now has a record that the fee was shopped — which is a useful fact if any beneficiary later asks why the legal bill was what it was.

Hire a lawyer for the legal work, not the clerical work. Know what the lawyer should and shouldn't bill you for. Choose carefully, in writing, with a clear fee structure. Manage the relationship actively — written questions, batched communication, careful bill review. Switch if it's not working. You're the executor. The lawyer works for the estate, through you.

CHAPTER 9

Distributing Assets the Right Way

Chapter at a Glance

- Reading the will carefully — specific, general, and residuary bequests.
- What happens when there's no will (intestate succession).
- Preliminary distribution: when it's safe and when it isn't.
- The exact sequence for the final distribution.
- Why a signed release from each beneficiary is your single best protection.

Distribution is the part everyone has been waiting for — and the part that ends a lot of friendships if it's done wrong. This chapter is about how to do it cleanly, with documentation that protects you and a process that keeps the family on the same page.

The basic order: you finish the inventory, you pay the debts and taxes, you wait out the creditor window, you give beneficiaries a preliminary accounting, you distribute, and you collect signed receipts. Then you go back to the court to close the estate.

> **KEY POINT**
>
> Don't distribute too early. Distributing before creditors are handled is one of the fastest ways for an executor to end up personally liable. The creditor-claim window exists for a reason. Wait it out.

Read the Will Carefully

Before you distribute a single thing, read the will again. Slowly. With a highlighter.

You're looking for three categories of provision:

1. **Specific bequests** — "my grandmother's pearls to my daughter Sarah," "my collection of model trains to my nephew Tom." These are particular items going to particular people.
2. **General bequests** — "$10,000 to my best friend Linda," "$5,000 to the local food bank." These are amounts of money going to particular people or institutions.
3. **The residuary** — "the rest, residue, and remainder of my estate." This is everything else, going to whoever the will names as the residuary beneficiary or beneficiaries (often "my children, in equal shares").

Specific bequests go first. General bequests go next. The residuary is what's left after everything above plus all debts and taxes have been satisfied. If the estate isn't big enough to cover specific and general bequests in full, they get reduced pro rata or by formula the will specifies (this is called "abatement").

What If There's No Will?

If the deceased died without a will ("intestate"), the state has default rules for who inherits. The exact rules vary state by state but the broad outlines are similar:

- **Spouse only, no kids:** spouse gets everything.
- **Spouse and kids of that spouse:** typically spouse gets a substantial share (often everything, sometimes half), kids get the rest.
- **Spouse and kids from a previous relationship:** more complicated. Spouse usually gets a smaller share; the deceased's kids from the prior relationship get the rest. This is where most family fights start.
- **No spouse, kids only:** kids split equally.
- **No spouse, no kids:** parents inherit if living; if not, siblings; if not, nieces and nephews; further out from there.
- **No living relatives:** the state inherits (called "escheat"). This is rare but legally real.

If you're administering an intestate estate, your county's probate court usually has a one-page summary of your state's intestate-succession rules. Get a copy. Make sure your distributions match exactly. Mistakes in intestate distribution are common and lead to personal liability for the executor.

Preliminary Distribution — Should You Do One?

Sometimes beneficiaries genuinely need money before the estate is closed. A spouse who needs to keep paying the mortgage. A child whose tuition is due. A beneficiary in financial hardship.

Preliminary distributions are allowed in most states, but they're risky for you. The risk: if you distribute money and later a creditor presents a valid claim that empties the remaining estate, you're personally on the hook to claw back the distribution. If the beneficiary has spent the money, you may be writing a check from your own bank account.

Two protections that reduce the risk:

1. **Wait out the creditor-claim window first.** Most states have a four-to-six-month window after publication. Don't distribute anything substantial before it closes.
2. **Get a court order authorizing the distribution.** This adds time and a small filing fee, but it shifts the risk: the court has approved the distribution as reasonable, and you're protected if it later turns out to have been premature.

If you distribute without court approval and a problem arises, you can ask the beneficiary to return the money. Sometimes they do. Sometimes they can't. You absorb the difference.

Final Distribution — The Right Sequence

Here's the order that protects you:

1. **Confirm all debts have been paid or are barred by the statute.** The creditor-claim window has closed. Tax returns have been filed. Any tax payments have cleared.
2. **Prepare the final accounting.** This is a complete record of every dollar in and out, every asset disposition, every fee paid, every distribution proposed. Most courts have a form.
3. **Send the final accounting to every beneficiary** before you distribute. Give them time to ask questions or object. 30 days is typical.
4. **File the accounting with the court** along with a petition to approve it and authorize distribution.
5. **Get the court's approval** — usually a hearing, sometimes just an order.
6. **Distribute** — issue checks, transfer titles, hand over personal property.
7. **Collect signed receipts and releases** from each beneficiary acknowledging what they received and releasing you from further claims.
8. **File the receipts with the court** and petition to close the estate.

9. **Receive the court's order closing the estate.** You are discharged.

Receipts and Releases — Don't Skip These

Every beneficiary, before you hand over their distribution, signs a document that says: "I, [Name], have received [amount or items] from the Estate of [Deceased]. I acknowledge that this is my full distribution. I release the executor from any further claims related to the administration of this estate."

The release is your protection. Without it, a beneficiary can come back two years later and claim they didn't get what they were owed. With it, that argument is finished. Some states have specific release-form requirements; the probate attorney (if you have one) or the court will have a template.

If a beneficiary refuses to sign a release, you have two options: (1) hold their distribution and ask the court to compel a release, or (2) deposit their distribution with the court and let them claim it. Don't just hand over the money without a signed release.

In-Kind vs. Cash

Some inheritances are easy — money to a named person, item to a named person. Others are trickier — "split my brokerage account 60/40 between my two children."

Two approaches:

- **In-kind:** transfer the actual securities. Open a new account for each beneficiary at the same brokerage, transfer the agreed-upon percentage of each holding into each account, and you're done. Advantage: no taxable event from a sale. Disadvantage: the beneficiaries have to manage what they got.
- **Cash:** sell everything, deposit the proceeds in the estate account, and write checks. Advantage: cleaner accounting and simpler distribution. Disadvantage: potential capital-gains tax on appreciated securities (though step-up in basis at death usually minimizes this).

Talk to a CPA before you choose. The decision usually depends on the specific tax basis of the assets, the cash needs of the beneficiaries, and how amicable the family is about handling investments themselves.

> **KEY POINT**
>
> DO THIS NOW — Before any distribution, write out the proposed distribution to each beneficiary on a single page: "Beneficiary A receives [X]. Beneficiary B receives [Y]. Beneficiary C receives [Z]." Send it to every beneficiary 30 days before distribution. If anyone objects, you find out now, not after the checks have cleared.

What This Looks Like in Practice

When the estate was ready to close, David sent each of the four beneficiaries a one-page distribution plan. It listed: their name, what they were getting (specific items, dollar amount, or both), and the date he proposed to distribute (thirty days from the date of the letter).

Three of the four beneficiaries signed and returned the acknowledgement within a week. The fourth, his cousin Patricia, wrote back to say she was "not satisfied" with her share.

David called her. They talked for forty minutes. Patricia wasn't actually disputing the will's math — she just wanted to be heard. By the end of the call, she had no specific objection to file. David sent her the release to sign. She signed it the following Tuesday.

Had David tried to hand Patricia her distribution check before that conversation, she would have refused to sign the release. Without the release, David would have had to either deposit her share with the court or hold it indefinitely. The forty-minute call was the cheapest estate-administration expense David incurred.

What This Chapter Has Said

Notes from Real Estates

The release is the entire end-game. Without a signed release from each beneficiary, you remain personally on the hook for that distribution indefinitely. With one, you're discharged. The release isn't optional — it's the legal end of your responsibility to that beneficiary.

If a beneficiary refuses to sign, deposit their share with the court and let them claim it. The court holds the funds, the beneficiary appears, signs the release at the courthouse, and walks out with the money. You are out of the loop. This is not a punishment — it's a standard procedure that most counties handle routinely.

Distributing in-kind versus in cash is a real decision. In-kind means transferring actual securities (or property) to beneficiaries in their existing form. It avoids a sale event. It's often the right answer for appreciated securities, where the basis step-up at death is preserved. In cash means selling and writing checks. Cleaner accounting. Simpler distribution.

Talk to a CPA before you choose. The answer often surprises people who haven't thought about basis carefully.

Patterns That Repeat

Pattern: the surprise residuary beneficiary

The residuary clause — "the rest, residue, and remainder of my estate, I leave to..." — is the cleanup provision that catches everything not specifically given away. In many wills, it's where most of the estate actually goes.

A common pattern: the will gives specific items to specific people (the watch to a grandchild, $5,000 to a charity, the car to a son), and then leaves "the rest" to the surviving spouse or to children in equal shares. Beneficiaries who got specific items often think they're the "main" inheritors. They're often not.

The residuary beneficiary frequently gets the bulk of the value.

Read the will carefully. Map who gets what. Don't assume the order of names in the will reflects the proportions of value.

Pattern: the in-kind distribution of appreciated stock

If the deceased held individual stocks that have appreciated significantly, the basis step-up at death resets each holding's cost basis to the fair market value on the date of death. Distributing in-kind to beneficiaries preserves that step-up.

If you sell the stock inside the estate and then distribute cash, the estate pays capital-gains tax on any appreciation between the date of death and the sale date. For volatile or appreciating positions, in-kind distribution is usually the better answer. Talk to a CPA before you sell anything significant.

Pattern: the disclaimer that reshapes the inheritance

A beneficiary can legally refuse part or all of an inheritance through a written disclaimer filed within nine months of the date of death. The disclaimed share then passes as if that beneficiary had died first — to the contingent beneficiary, or per the will's residuary clause, or per state intestacy rules.

Disclaimers are common when an adult child is already wealthy and would rather see the share pass to their own children, or when accepting the inheritance would trigger Medicaid recovery or other unintended consequences.

The disclaimer is not a tax-planning lever every beneficiary needs, but it is a tool every executor should know exists — and should mention to any beneficiary who might benefit.

Pattern: the partial distribution that calms the family

If administration is going to run a year or more — and most of them do — consider a partial distribution at the six-month mark. Pay out a reasonable share of the cash on hand to the residuary beneficiaries, reserving enough for remaining taxes, fees, and contingencies.

The court usually permits this without a formal hearing, with a simple interim accounting.

Figure 9.1

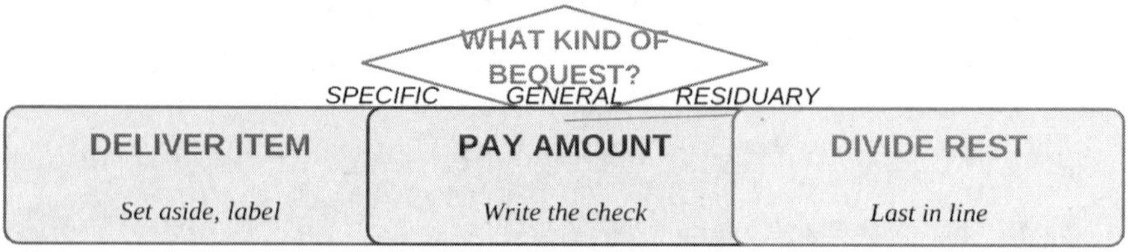

How the will distributes — specific bequests, general bequests, and the residuary that catches everything else.

Partial distributions reduce family tension by demonstrating progress. They also make the final distribution easier — the math is already largely done. Talk to the attorney about the reserve amount before issuing checks; the reserve protects you personally if a late creditor claim surfaces.

Read the will carefully and follow it. Pay debts first, then specific and general bequests, then the residuary. Wait out the creditor window before distributing anything substantial. Use the formal sequence: accounting, beneficiary review, court approval, distribution, signed releases, court discharge. Don't hand over money without a release. Don't distribute too early.

Done right, this protects you and ends the estate cleanly.

PART 4

PROTECTION

What goes wrong, why, and how to keep yourself out of trouble.

CHAPTER 10

Common Mistakes Executors Make

Chapter at a Glance

- The eleven recurring mistakes executors make.
- Why most of them are made in good faith.
- The specific cure for each — administrative, not catastrophic.
- How to catch yourself before a small slip becomes a big problem.
- The one mistake that is harder to fix than the rest.

Most estates that end badly do so because of a handful of specific mistakes — almost always made in good faith. Here are the eleven we see most often, with the cure for each.

Read this chapter before you make any of these mistakes. Read it again if you think you might have made one already — most of them have a fix if you catch them in time.

Mistake 1: Mixing Estate Money with Your Own

What it looks like: paying for a funeral expense on your personal credit card, intending to reimburse yourself later. Cashing a check made out to the deceased and putting it into your personal account. Selling the deceased's car and depositing the proceeds with your own savings.

Why it's bad: it's the single fastest way to get hit with a breach-of-duty claim. Even if you eventually pay yourself back and the books balance, you've commingled funds. Courts and beneficiaries get suspicious. Suspicion turns into accusations. Accusations turn into legal exposure.

The fix: open the estate bank account immediately after appointment. Run every transaction through it. Reimburse yourself only with documented receipts, by check from the estate account to your personal account, with a notation showing what each reimbursement was for.

Mistake 2: Distributing Too Early

What it looks like: handing a beneficiary their share before the creditor-claim window has closed. Distributing personal property before the inventory is complete. Writing checks before the estate has paid debts and taxes.

Why it's bad: if a creditor surfaces after distribution and the remaining estate can't cover the claim, the executor is personally liable to claw back the distribution. If the beneficiary has spent the money, you may be paying out of your own pocket.

The fix: wait out the creditor-claim window. File a final accounting. Get court approval. Only then distribute.

Mistake 3: Ignoring the Creditor-Notice Requirements

What it looks like: skipping the newspaper publication because "we know who the creditors are." Not sending direct notice to known creditors. Hoping the bills will just stop coming.

Why it's bad: without proper notice, the creditor-claim window doesn't close. Creditors can come knocking years later. The estate stays technically open. Beneficiaries who got distributions may have to give them back.

The fix: do both notice steps — newspaper publication and direct written notice to known creditors. Document both. The $100 you spend on the newspaper notice is the cheapest insurance you'll buy.

Mistake 4: Not Filing the Tax Returns

What it looks like: forgetting that the deceased's final income-tax return (for the year they died) is due April 15 of the following year. Not filing the estate's own income-tax return (for income the estate earned during administration). Missing the federal estate-tax return deadline (nine months after death, with extensions available).

Why it's bad: late-filing penalties and interest mount fast. And the IRS doesn't write off penalties because "the executor didn't realize."

The fix: identify the tax returns required for your situation in the first month. Hire a CPA who does estate work. Calendar the deadlines. Most estates need at least: the deceased's final 1040 (due April 15 of year after death), and the estate's 1041s for any year the estate is open and earning income.

Mistake 5: Favoring One Beneficiary

What it looks like: letting one sibling have a few items before distribution "because she needed them." Communicating more with the beneficiaries you like. Bending the will's terms to make a beneficiary happy.

Why it's bad: the duty to treat beneficiaries impartially is not optional. Even small favoritism — perceived or actual — destroys trust and invites the disfavored beneficiaries to challenge everything you do.

The fix: send the same letter, the same accounting, the same update, on the same day, to every beneficiary. Treat them all as equally entitled to information. If one needs an answer, send the answer to all of them simultaneously.

Mistake 6: Acting Without Authority

What it looks like: signing documents "as executor" before the court has formally appointed you. Cleaning out the house and donating items before the inventory is complete. Selling an asset before authorized.

Why it's bad: without court appointment, you have no legal authority to act. Anything you sign isn't binding. Anything you sell may be undone. You may be personally liable.

The fix: wait until the court issues your Letters Testamentary before you exercise executor authority. In the gap between death and appointment (typically 30–90 days), focus on securing and preserving — not selling, distributing, or committing the estate.

Mistake 7: Bad Recordkeeping

What it looks like: trying to reconstruct months of transactions from memory. Losing receipts. Estimating values instead of documenting them. Not logging time spent.

Why it's bad: the court will ask for an accounting. Beneficiaries will ask. Reconstructing later is painful, incomplete, and looks suspicious. Missing documentation is what enables "prove it" challenges from disgruntled beneficiaries.

The fix: log every transaction the day it happens or the week it happens. Use a spreadsheet. Photograph receipts. Save bank and brokerage statements in a folder. Ten minutes a week now saves a hundred hours later.

Mistake 8: Selling Assets to Family Below Market

What it looks like: letting a sibling "buy" the deceased's car for $1. Selling the family home to a beneficiary for less than the appraised value. Letting a beneficiary keep something and "call it part of their share" without independent valuation.

Why it's bad: every transaction with a beneficiary creates a potential conflict-of-interest claim from the other beneficiaries. Below-market sales raise the question: "Why did the executor give a sweetheart deal to her?"

The fix: get an arm's-length appraisal on any significant asset. Either sell at appraised value or get unanimous written beneficiary consent in advance for any below-market sale. Document everything.

Mistake 9: Skipping the Final Accounting

What it looks like: distributing the assets and considering the estate "done" without filing the final accounting and petition to close. Assuming the court will figure out it's over.

Why it's bad: the estate technically stays open. The executor remains liable. Beneficiaries can later claim distributions were wrong because no formal closing protected them. Creditors have an indefinite window if proper notice wasn't given and the case wasn't closed.

The fix: file the final accounting. File the petition to close. Get the order discharging you as executor. This is the legal end of your obligation. Without it, you're still on the hook.

Mistake 10: Forgetting the Beneficiary Designations

What it looks like: treating the 401(k) as part of the probate estate when it has a named beneficiary. Trying to distribute the life insurance through the will when there's a named beneficiary. Misunderstanding which assets go through probate and which don't.

Why it's bad: assets with named beneficiaries (retirement accounts, life insurance, payable-on-death accounts, transfer-on-death accounts) skip the estate entirely. Trying to bring them into the estate creates tax problems for the beneficiary and delays the distribution they should have received directly.

The fix: in the first month, identify every account with a named beneficiary. Notify each custodian of the death. Provide the named beneficiary's contact info to the custodian. Step aside from those assets — they go to the beneficiary directly, not through you.

Mistake 11: Not Saying No

What it looks like: agreeing to be executor for a friend because you couldn't say no at the funeral. Agreeing to handle an estate you don't have time for. Continuing to serve when your own life has fallen apart.

Why it's bad: half-attending to executor duties is worse than declining. Estates dragged out for years by overcommitted executors are the most common cause of family bitterness and the second most common cause of beneficiary lawsuits.

The fix: decline before appointment, or resign after, if you genuinely can't do this. There's no shame in it. A professional administrator, a successor named in the will, or a court-appointed replacement will do better than an overwhelmed family member doing it half-attentively.

> **KEY POINT**
>
> DO THIS NOW — Read the list of eleven mistakes again. Mark the ones you might already be slipping toward. For each, write down the specific fix you're going to apply this week. Most of these are reversible if caught early.

What This Looks Like in Practice

Brad's first instinct, after being appointed executor of his uncle's estate, was to pay things from his own account and reimburse himself later. The funeral home, the locksmith, the storage facility — all on his personal credit card.

When his sister, also a beneficiary, asked for an accounting six weeks in, Brad couldn't easily produce one. The expenses were scattered across his credit-card statement, mixed in with his own grocery and gas purchases. He spent four hours over a weekend reconstructing what he'd spent on the estate and what he'd spent on himself.

His sister was understanding. The probate attorney was less so — he sat Brad down and explained that commingling executor funds was the single fastest way to invite a breach-of-duty claim.

Brad immediately opened the estate account, transferred the documented reimbursable amounts from his personal account into it via a single labeled transaction, and from that day forward ran every dollar through the estate account.

The estate eventually closed cleanly. But the four hours of reconstructing — plus the small embarrassment of being corrected by his attorney — were entirely avoidable. The fix was the EIN, the estate account, and the discipline of running everything through it.

What This Chapter Has Said

Notes from Real Estates

Mistakes 1 and 7 are the same mistake. Mixing money and bad records are the two faces of the same failure: you don't have one clear source of truth for where the estate's money lives and what's happened to it.

The cure for both is the same: open the estate account immediately, run everything through it, and log every transaction in the same place.

Mistakes 2, 6, and 8 are about acting before you're ready. Distributing too early. Acting without authority. Selling below market. All three come from the same impulse — wanting to move things along, get the work done, see results. Resist. The slow, documented, authorized path is the safe path. The fast path is the path that produces personal liability.

Mistake 11 is the most underrated. Not saying no. Agreeing to be executor for someone you have no time or temperament to do this job for. Half-attending to the duties because you said yes out of loyalty but really couldn't do it well.

That mistake is harder to fix than any of the others because by the time you realize, you're the one who said yes. Declining before appointment is almost always the right call when you're uncertain.

Patterns That Repeat

Pattern: the executor who realizes they've made a mistake

Most executors who realize they've made a mistake don't react well. They get defensive. They try to hide it. They hope no one will notice. All three reactions make the problem worse.

The right reaction is the opposite. Tell the probate attorney (or hire one if you haven't) immediately. Document what happened in a brief written note to yourself dated that day. If a beneficiary or creditor is affected, communicate transparently — "I want to flag a specific issue with how I handled X. Here's what happened.

Here's how I'm correcting it." Almost every executor mistake is fixable if caught early. Almost every executor mistake becomes serious only when concealed.

Pattern: the slow build of small failures

Most estate administrations that end badly don't fail because of one big mistake. They fail because of an accumulation of small ones: a few transactions not logged, one beneficiary kept slightly more in the loop than the others, a creditor notice sent slightly late, a tax deadline missed by a few days. Each individually is recoverable.

Together they create an impression of carelessness that, by month nine, has hardened into suspicion.

Figure 10.1

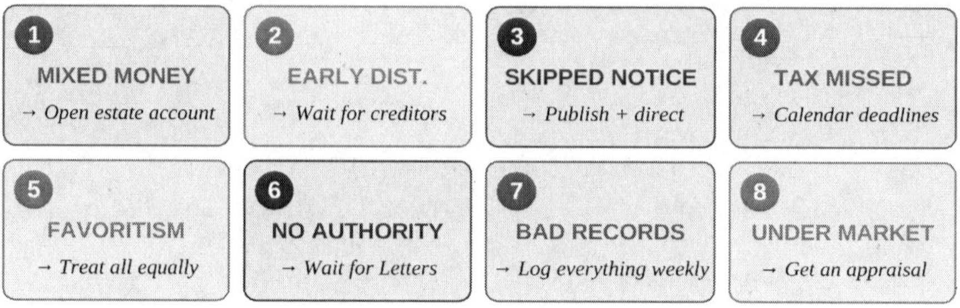

Eight of the eleven recurring executor mistakes — and the specific cure for each.

The cure for the slow build is the weekly check-in. Spend twenty minutes every Sunday reviewing what you did the previous week, what you owe for the coming week, and whether anything has slipped. The discipline of the weekly check-in catches every small drift before it becomes a pattern.

Estate problems come from a small set of recurring mistakes — mixing money, distributing too early, skipping notice, missing tax returns, favoring beneficiaries, acting without authority, bad records, below-market family sales, no final accounting, forgetting beneficiary designations, and not saying no. Each has a specific cure if caught early. Most are administrative, not catastrophic.

Knowing what to watch for is most of the battle.

PART 5

◆

ACTION

The timeline, month by month — and the final checklist that closes the estate.

CHAPTER 11

Simple Timeline to Follow

Chapter at a Glance

- A clean month-by-month playbook for the typical estate.
- What to do in month 1, month 2, and so on through month 12.
- What the typical close looks like (9–15 months).
- Common reasons the timeline slips and what to do.
- The shape of the work, so you always know what's next.

Most estates close in nine to fifteen months. Some take longer for legitimate reasons — contested wills, complex businesses, real estate in multiple states. Some take longer for preventable reasons — bad recordkeeping, missed deadlines, an executor who can't say no to family demands.

This chapter is a month-by-month walkthrough of what you should be doing. Use it as a checklist. Use it as a calendar. Use it as a sanity check when you wonder whether things are on track.

KEY POINT

The timeline below assumes an average estate without major complications. Your specific situation may run faster (smaller estates often close in six months) or slower (contested wills can take years). Adjust accordingly, but keep the sequence — the order of operations matters even when the calendar shifts.

Month 1 — Confirm, Secure, Find

Already covered in Chapters 1–4. The headlines:

- Confirm the death; arrange the funeral.
- Secure the home (locks, mail, perishables, thermostat, photographs).
- Find the will and key documents.
- Order 8–10 certified death certificates.
- Identify and notify the immediate critical parties (Social Security, employer, credit bureaus).
- Make a rough list of assets and where they are.
- Decide whether to accept appointment as executor.

By the end of month 1: you have the will, you know roughly what the estate contains, and the immediate identity-theft and asset-loss risks are handled.

Month 2 — Open Probate and the Estate Account

This is the month the formal process starts. Tasks:

- File the petition for probate with the county probate court.

- Submit the will and any required affidavits.
- Attend the appointment hearing (often a brief proceeding) and receive your Letters Testamentary.
- Apply for the estate's EIN (online, free, ten minutes at IRS.gov).
- Open the estate bank account.
- Notify all financial institutions formally with copies of the death certificate and Letters.
- Send the beneficiary notification letter (Chapter 5).
- Publish notice to creditors in the local newspaper.
- Send direct written notice to known creditors.
- Engage a CPA who handles estate work; book a planning conversation.
- Engage a probate attorney if the estate requires one (Chapter 8).

By the end of month 2: you're formally appointed, the estate account is open, the notifications are sent, and the creditor clock has started.

Months 3–4 — Inventory and Valuation

Now the heavy lifting on assets begins:

- Complete the formal inventory of estate assets. Most courts require it filed within 60–90 days of appointment.

- Get appraisals: real estate, jewelry, art, collectibles, vehicles, business interests.
- Collect and consolidate financial accounts into the estate account or under estate control. Brokerages will require certified copies of Letters Testamentary to transfer or sell.
- Begin handling routine bills from the estate account.
- Process and review creditor claims as they come in. Approve, deny, or negotiate each one.
- Continue managing real estate — mortgage payments, taxes, insurance, maintenance.
- Begin preliminary work on the deceased's final income-tax return (Chapter 6).

By the end of month 4: every asset has a documented value, the inventory is filed with the court, and routine administration is humming along.

Months 5–6 — Process Claims, File Returns

The middle phase:

- Most states' creditor-claim windows close around month 5 or 6. Confirm yours.
- Pay valid claims in priority order. Deny invalid claims in writing.
- File the deceased's final income-tax return (Form 1040). For most people this is due April 15 of the year after death; if death was in early in the calendar year, this may fall

during this window.

- Begin work on the estate's first income-tax return (Form 1041) if the estate has had income during administration.
- If federal or state estate tax applies, begin work on those returns. The federal return is generally due nine months after death (extensions available).
- Hold any necessary discussions with beneficiaries about specific items they hope to receive. Document agreements.
- If real estate will be sold, list it during this window so the sale can close by month 8 or 9.

By the end of month 6: creditor claims are mostly resolved, tax returns are in progress or filed, and you have a clear picture of what's left for distribution.

Months 7–9 — Resolve, Sell, Prepare to Close

Wrapping up the work:

- Complete any pending asset sales. Deposit proceeds in the estate account.
- Pay any remaining bills, taxes, and approved claims.
- Reconcile the estate account; verify every transaction is documented.
- If a beneficiary is requesting a preliminary distribution, evaluate (Chapter 9) and either decline or seek court approval.
- Begin drafting the final accounting.

- Communicate the projected final timeline and distribution amounts to beneficiaries.

By the end of month 9: most estates are within striking distance of closing. Final accounting is drafted. Distribution plan is set.

Months 10–12 — Close the Estate

The final stretch:

- Send the final accounting to every beneficiary. Allow 30 days for review and questions.
- File the final accounting with the court along with the petition to approve and distribute.
- Attend the closing hearing if one is scheduled.
- Once authorized, distribute: write the checks, transfer the titles, hand over the personal property.
- Collect signed receipts and releases from each beneficiary.
- File the receipts with the court.
- Petition for and receive the order discharging you as executor.
- Close the estate bank account once all distributions have cleared.
- Keep estate records for at least seven years.

By the end of month 12 — or month 15 in slower jurisdictions — you are discharged. The estate is closed. The legal and financial chapter of your loved one's life is complete.

When the Timeline Slips

Common reasons the timeline runs long, and what to do:

- **Real estate doesn't sell.** Re-list at a lower price, rent it temporarily and distribute it later, or distribute it in-kind to a beneficiary who wants it.
- **A creditor claim is contested.** Pursue resolution through the court. Don't let it freeze the rest of the administration.
- **A will contest is filed.** This is a separate legal proceeding that can take a year or more. Continue with the rest of the administration in parallel if the court allows; otherwise hold and let the litigation resolve.
- **Tax returns are delayed.** Get the CPA on a hard deadline. Tax-related delays are the most common preventable slowdown.
- **A beneficiary refuses to sign a release.** Deposit their distribution with the court or seek a compulsory release. Don't let a single holdout prevent the close.

> **KEY POINT**
>
> DO THIS NOW — Pull out a calendar. Find the month of death. From there, mark month 2, month 4, month 6, month 9, and month 12. Write the headline for each month next to the date. This is your timeline. Check back monthly.

What This Looks Like in Practice

Karen's father died on March 4. Here's what her timeline actually looked like.

- **March:** funeral, secured home, found will, located trust documents.
- **April:** filed probate, got appointed, opened the estate account, sent beneficiary letters, published creditor notice.
- **May–June:** completed inventory, got appraisals on real estate and jewelry, notified all institutions, began processing creditor claims.
- **July–August:** paid valid claims, denied two invalid claims in writing, filed father's final 1040, prepped the brokerage for distribution.
- **September:** listed the family home; closed in early November.
- **October–November:** reconciled estate account, drafted final accounting, sent distribution plan to all beneficiaries.
- **December:** all beneficiaries signed releases; final accounting filed with court.

- **January (10 months in):** court signed order discharging Karen as executor. Estate closed.

Karen described the work afterward as "a part-time job for ten months." She estimated 250 hours total — about an hour a day, with heavier weeks in months 2, 3, 6, and 11. She was glad it was over. She also said she'd do it again if asked. "Now I know how."

What This Chapter Has Said

Notes from Real Estates

The timeline shifts but the sequence doesn't. Some estates close in six months. Some take three years. The specific dates move. But you always have to: confirm death first, get appointed before opening accounts, inventory before selling, give notice before paying, file returns before closing, get court approval before distributing, get releases before discharge.

The order is what produces a clean close.

Estates that drift past 15 months almost always do so for one of four reasons. A will contest. A complicated business or real-estate situation. A beneficiary who won't sign a release. Or — most preventable — an executor who never quite gets around to filing the final accounting. Of the four, the last is the one fully within your control.

Don't be that executor.

The closing hearing is almost always uneventful. Judges have seen hundreds of these. If your accounting is complete, your distribution plan is reasonable, and your beneficiaries have signed releases, the hearing is short — ten minutes, sometimes less. Show up prepared, answer questions clearly, and walk out with the discharge.

Patterns That Repeat

Pattern: the month-6 wall

Around month six, most executors hit a wall. The novelty of the work has worn off. The end is still months away. The beneficiaries are restless. The creditor claims are mostly handled but the closing process feels far off.

This is normal. It is also the moment to keep your head down and grind through. The work itself is actually getting easier — most of the chaos of months 2–5 is behind you, and the closing of months 10–12 is structured and clear. The middle is just the middle. Trust the timeline. Show up to your weekly check-in.

The wall passes.

Pattern: the asset that won't sell

Some estates carry a real-estate parcel, a business interest, or a collectible that simply won't sell at the appraised value. The market shifted. The buyers disappeared. The condition is worse than the appraisal assumed.

Figure 11.1

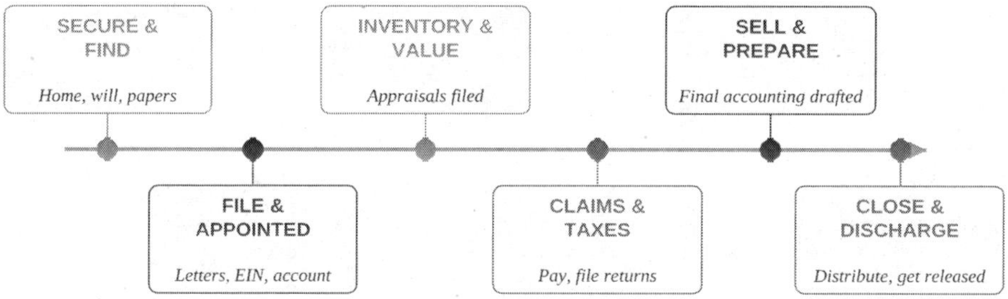

The executor's twelve-month timeline — from death to discharge, month by month.

Three options: lower the price (and accept that the estate gets less than expected), distribute the asset in-kind to a beneficiary who's willing to take it at the current valuation, or hold it (if the will allows) and let the residuary beneficiary inherit the obligation to sell. The first is usually fastest. The second is often fairest.

The third only works if everyone agrees and the will doesn't require sale.

Most estates close in nine to fifteen months on a predictable sequence: confirm and secure (month 1), open probate (month 2), inventory and value (months 3–4), process claims and file returns (months 5–6), resolve and prepare to close (months 7–9), final accounting and distribution (months 10–12). Slips happen but most have fixes. The sequence matters even when the calendar moves.

CHAPTER 12

Final Checklist: Closing the Estate

Chapter at a Glance

- What goes in the final accounting (and what doesn't).
- The distribution plan, sent to beneficiaries 30 days before distribution.
- Receipts and releases — your single best protection.
- The court approval and discharge order that legally ends the job.
- The 20-item one-page closing checklist.

If you've made it to this chapter, the estate is almost done. This chapter is the last sixty days, laid out as a single checklist you can tear out (or photocopy) and work through item by item.

Some items will already be complete. Some will surface as you go through the list. The point is to have one consolidated view of what "done" looks like.

> **KEY POINT**
>
> Closing the estate is not the same as distributing the assets. Distribution comes first; the formal close comes after, when the court signs the order discharging you. The discharge is what protects you from later claims. Don't skip it.

Final Accounting — What Goes In It

The accounting is a complete record. It includes:

1. **Opening inventory** — every asset the estate started with, with date-of-death values.
2. **Receipts** — every dollar that came into the estate during administration: refunds, sale proceeds, investment income, recovered overpayments.
3. **Disbursements** — every dollar that went out: bills paid, debts settled, fees, taxes, executor compensation, attorney and CPA fees.
4. **Distributions** — what each beneficiary received (or is about to receive).
5. **Ending balance** — what's left in the estate account at the moment of closing. This should be zero or near it once distributions are complete.
6. **Supporting documentation** — copies of canceled checks, receipts, appraisals, sale documents, tax returns.

Most courts have a specific form. Use it. If the form isn't a perfect fit for your situation, attach a narrative explanation. Better to over-document than under-.

The Final Distribution Plan

Along with the accounting, you'll submit a distribution plan. It's straightforward:

- Each beneficiary's name.
- What they're receiving — exact dollar amount, or specific items, or both.
- How it's being delivered — check, wire transfer, in-kind transfer of securities, hand-delivery of personal property.
- Total distribution per beneficiary, verifying it matches the will's provisions.

Send this plan to every beneficiary 30 days before you distribute. Give them time to question or object. Then file it with the court along with the accounting.

Releases — One Per Beneficiary

Before any beneficiary receives their distribution, they sign a release. The basic template:

> **RECEIPT AND RELEASE**
>
> "I, [Beneficiary Name], acknowledge receipt of [specific items or amount] from the Estate of [Deceased], representing my full share under the terms of the will dated [date]. I have reviewed the final accounting and approve it. I release the executor, [Executor Name], from any further claims arising from the administration of the estate. Dated: [date]. Signed: [Beneficiary Name]."

Each beneficiary signs their own. Witness or notarize per state rules. File all releases with the court along with your petition to close.

Court Approval and the Final Hearing

In most states, closing the estate requires a final court filing — sometimes a hearing, sometimes just an order on the papers. The petition asks the court to:

- Approve the final accounting.
- Authorize the final distributions.
- Approve any final fees (executor compensation, attorney, CPA).
- Discharge the executor.
- Close the case.

If there's a hearing, attend in person or by phone. The judge may have specific questions. Have your documents handy. The hearing is usually short — fifteen to thirty minutes for an uncontested closing.

If the closing is on the papers (no hearing), the order comes back signed within a few weeks. File it with the estate records and you're done.

The Sixty-Day Closing Checklist

Here is the checklist in single-page form:

1. All creditor claims paid, denied, or barred by deadline. [ ]

2. All taxes filed: final 1040, any estate 1041s, federal Form 706 if required, state returns. [ ]

3. All asset sales complete and proceeds in the estate account. [ ]

4. All bank and brokerage accounts consolidated or distributed. [ ]

5. Real estate sold, transferred, or queued for distribution. [ ]

6. Personal property inventoried, distributed per plan, with signed receipts. [ ]

7. Estate account reconciled; every transaction documented. [ ]

8. Final accounting drafted and reviewed. [ ]

9. Distribution plan drafted. [ ]

10. Final accounting and distribution plan sent to every beneficiary (30 days before closing). [ ]

11. Beneficiary questions answered, objections (if any) resolved. [ ]

12. Final accounting filed with the court. [ ]

13. Court hearing attended or order received. [ ]

14. Distributions made: checks issued, titles transferred, items delivered. [ ]

15. Receipts and releases signed by every beneficiary. [ ]

16. Receipts filed with the court. [ ]
17. Order of discharge received from the court. [ ]
18. Estate bank account closed. [ ]
19. EIN closed with the IRS. [ ]
20. Estate records archived (keep at least 7 years). [ ]

When the last box is checked, you are done. The job is complete.

After You're Discharged

A few cleanup items:

- Keep the estate records in a labeled box or folder for at least seven years. Tax authorities can audit; beneficiaries can question. The records are your defense.
- If you took executor compensation, report it on your personal tax return for the year you received it. Your CPA can advise on the specific category.
- Send a final brief note to the beneficiaries: "The estate is closed. The court has discharged me. Thank you for your patience." One paragraph, simple, warm. It ends the relationship cleanly.
- Reflect, if you want to, on what you learned. You just managed something most adults never have to. The next person who asks you to be executor will have a much easier time of it because of what you now know.

> **KEY POINT**
>
> DO THIS NOW — When the discharge order arrives, frame the checklist above (with every box checked) and put it somewhere you can see it. You did a hard thing well. The acknowledgment is worth keeping.

What This Looks Like in Practice

Greg printed out the 20-item closing checklist and taped it to the side of his refrigerator in month 9. By month 11, every box was checked except the last four — court approval, distributions, releases, and the discharge.

On the morning of the closing hearing, the judge spent about ten minutes reviewing the final accounting and the distribution plan. She had two questions — one about a reimbursement Greg had claimed for mileage to and from the bank, one about a small unsecured debt that had been denied and barred. Greg answered both clearly.

The judge signed the order.

Distributions went out the following Monday. Releases came back within two weeks. The discharge order arrived by mail eleven days after that. Greg closed the estate bank account, archived the records in two banker's boxes in his basement, and sent a brief final note to the beneficiaries — "The estate is closed. The court has discharged me.

Thank you for your patience."

He took down the checklist from the refrigerator. He looked at the twenty checkmarks. Then he put the checklist into the top of one of the banker's boxes — not because he needed it anymore, but because he wanted it to be the first thing he saw if he ever opened the box again. Twenty checkmarks.

A real piece of work.

What This Chapter Has Said

Notes from Real Estates

Keep the records for seven years. Tax authorities can audit. Beneficiaries can challenge. A creditor you thought you'd resolved can resurface with a paperwork dispute. The estate's records — the inventory, the receipts, the accounting, the signed releases, the discharge order — are your defense against all of these.

Two banker's boxes in a basement, labeled with the deceased's name and the year of discharge, is sufficient. Don't shred until year eight.

Send the final thank-you note. One paragraph, sent to every beneficiary the week the discharge arrives. "The estate is closed. The court has discharged me. Thank you for your patience." That's the whole note.

It's a small thing. It also closes the relationship warmly. Most of the people who receive it write back to say thank you. A few write back with apologies for being difficult during the middle months. A few send small gifts. None of that is the point — but it's the right way to end the work.

Pick up the lesson. You now know more about being an executor than ninety-five percent of adult Americans. Use that knowledge twice: once now, in the weeks of rest after the discharge, to recover.

And once later, quietly, for your own affairs — so that the person you name as your own executor someday has a much easier time of it than you did. That is the secret gift of having done this work. The next family in your circle starts further ahead.

Patterns That Repeat

Pattern: the beneficiary who delays signing the release

One beneficiary will sign the release within a week. One will sign in two weeks. One will sign in three. The fourth may sit on it for months. The cause is usually not the math; it's the emotional difficulty of acknowledging that the estate is closing and the deceased is really gone.

Give the beneficiary a deadline (gently): "I'd like to close the estate by [date]. Can you get the release back to me by [two weeks before]?" If they miss the deadline, deposit their distribution with the court and let them claim it on their own timeline. Don't let a single holdout prevent the close.

The court has procedures for exactly this.

Pattern: the discharge order that arrives without fanfare

After all the work — the months of accounting, the hearings, the distributions, the releases — the discharge order usually arrives by mail without ceremony. A single sheet of paper. A judge's signature. "The above-named executor is hereby discharged from further duties."

That's the end. There's no ceremony. There's no thank-you letter from the court. Just a piece of paper that, in exchange for ten or twelve months of careful work, ends your legal obligation. Frame it if you want. Or just file it in the estate records and close the box.

Either way, you did the work. The work mattered. And you're free.

Pattern: the next time someone asks

After your discharge, you'll find yourself in a different category of adult. You know what executor work actually involves. Friends who get the same call will ask you questions. Family members who hadn't thought about their own wills will start thinking about them. You become, without trying, the person in your circle who has done this.

Some of that you'll want to take on, and some you won't. Both are fine. If someone asks for advice, you can answer. If someone asks you to serve as their executor, you can decline — saying yes once doesn't obligate you to say yes again. The knowledge is portable. The obligation is not.

What is worth doing, quietly, is sharing what you learned. Recommend this book if it helped. Talk through the basics with family members who haven't yet faced this. Encourage them to draft a will, name an executor, and write a simple instruction letter that says where everything lives.

Figure 12.1

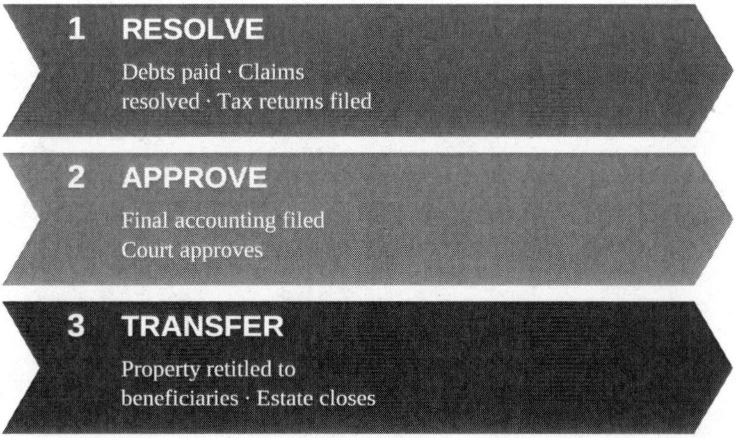

The closing sequence — resolve all claims, get court approval, transfer the assets, end the estate.

The work you just did was harder than it had to be, in part because the person who chose you didn't realize how much they could have eased it. Pay that forward.

Closing the estate is its own phase, separate from distribution. Prepare the final accounting. Send it to every beneficiary 30 days before closing. Get signed releases. File everything with the court. Receive the discharge order. Close the estate account. Archive the records. The checklist above is the single-page version.

When the last box is checked, the job is done — and you've done it well.

CONCLUSION

When the Last Box Is Checked

◆

Being executor is one of the more unusual things adult life asks of us. You probably didn't volunteer for it. Someone you cared about chose you, and you said yes because saying yes felt like loyalty.

And then the actual job began. Twelve months of paperwork, phone calls, careful records, family conversations, and small decisions that added up to one big result: the financial life of someone you loved was wound down with care, by someone they trusted, and the people they wanted to take care of got what they were supposed to get.

Not everyone gets that. Plenty of estates end with bitter siblings, depleted assets, missed deadlines, and lawsuits. The ones that don't are the ones where the executor took the job seriously, learned what they needed to learn, asked for help when they needed it, and kept good records.

That is what you have done.

The shape of the job hasn't changed since the first chapter — find, pay, distribute — but you now know what each of those actually means in practice. You know the difference between the assets that go through probate and the ones that don't. You know what the court expects and what it doesn't. You know how to talk to a lawyer without being run over by one. You know how to handle creditors, how to read the will carefully, and how to distribute with the documentation that ends the story cleanly.

If a future friend or family member asks you to be their executor, you will say yes from a different place. You'll know what you're agreeing to. You may even, quietly, be the one who makes it easy for the next family.

"Being a good executor is one of the most consequential things an ordinary person can do for the people they love."

It's not glamorous. Nobody throws an executor parade. The thanks you get, if you get any, are quiet — a hug from a sibling who didn't have to figure out the paperwork, a grandchild who got the heirloom intact, a spouse whose life didn't fall apart in the months after the funeral. Those small thanks are the whole point.

Take what you've learned and use it twice. Use it to do this job well. And then, when life slows back down, use it for yourself — your own will, your own plan, your own family. You now know what makes an executor's job easy. Make it easy for whoever you name next.

Take care of yours.

— AVOY Publishing

Spring 2026

READER FAQ

Common questions, organized by stage

◆

These are the questions readers ask most often, grouped by when they tend to ask them. Each answer is cross-referenced to the chapter that covers it in more depth.

The First Weeks

Do I have to accept being executor?

No. Until the court appoints you, you can file a one-page renunciation declining the role. The court will appoint the backup named in the will, or someone else if there is no backup. See Chapter 2.

Can I get reimbursed for funeral expenses I pay personally?

Yes, once you're appointed and the estate account is open, you reimburse yourself with documented receipts. Pay with a check or card you can document. Do not use the deceased's accounts. See Chapter 4.

Should I tell Social Security right away?

Yes. The funeral home usually files the report electronically. Confirm it was filed. SSA will pull back any payment for the month of death and after. See Chapter 5.

Can I move into the deceased's house while administering the estate?

Generally no, not without complications. If the house belongs to the estate, occupying it raises a fairness question with other beneficiaries. If you're going to do it, get the other beneficiaries' written agreement first and pay a fair rent into the estate. See Chapter 7.

The Middle Months

How long does this take?

Most estates close in nine to fifteen months. Faster for small, uncontested estates; longer for contested wills, complex businesses, or out-of-state real estate. See Chapter 11.

What if the will is missing?

Look in six common places (Chapter 3). If you can't find the original, you can sometimes file a copy with affidavits proving it existed and wasn't deliberately destroyed. If no copy exists either, the estate is administered as intestate — under state default rules. See Chapter 9.

A beneficiary is calling me constantly. What do I do?

Send the same monthly update to every beneficiary at the same time. When the calls happen, point them to the update. Don't negotiate the will's terms. Don't promise specific items or amounts. See Chapter 5.

Do I have to pay every bill that arrives?

No. Wait for creditors to present claims through the formal process. Many medical bills shrink dramatically after Medicare and other insurance reconciles. Many credit-card claims never get formally presented. See Chapter 6.

Closing the Estate

Do I need a lawyer to close the estate?

Not always. Simple estates can be closed with the court's self-help forms and a couple of hours of attorney consultation for specific questions. Complicated estates (contests, taxes, businesses, out-of-state property) need a lawyer. See Chapter 8.

How do I know when I'm officially done?

When the court signs an order discharging you as executor. Until then, you're still legally on the hook. After the discharge, the estate is closed and your obligation ends. See Chapter 12.

How long do I keep the estate records?

At least seven years. Tax authorities can audit. Beneficiaries can challenge years later. The records are your defense. See Chapter 12.

What if I made a mistake somewhere along the way?

Most mistakes are fixable if caught early. See Chapter 10 for the eleven most common ones and the specific cure for each. If you've already distributed and discover an error, talk to a probate attorney immediately. The longer you wait, the harder the fix.

GLOSSARY OF ESTATE TERMS

Plain-English definitions of every technical word in the book

◆

These are the words you'll hear from lawyers, banks, court clerks, and well-meaning family members during administration. Each definition is in plain language. If a word stops you in the chapters, the Glossary will start you again.

Administrator

Another name for executor — specifically used when there's no will and the court appoints someone to handle the estate. Same job either way.

Beneficiary

Someone named in the will (or under state default rules) to receive part of the estate.

Bequest

A gift in a will. "Specific bequest" = a particular item or amount to a particular person. "General bequest" = a dollar amount. "Residuary bequest" = whatever is left after specific and general bequests and debts are paid.

Codicil

A formal amendment to a will. Treated like a mini-will for validity purposes.

Decedent

The legal term for the deceased person. Mostly used in court paperwork.

Estate

Everything the deceased owned at death plus everything the estate earns during administration, minus what passes outside probate (joint property, POD/TOD accounts, retirement accounts with named beneficiaries, life insurance with named beneficiaries).

Executor

Also called personal representative, also called administrator (same job, different state names). See the WHAT IS AN EXECUTOR? callout in the Preface for the full definition.

Fiduciary

Someone legally required to act in another's best interest, not their own. Executors are fiduciaries to the estate and the beneficiaries.

Gross Estate

The total value of everything the deceased owned at death, before debts and expenses are subtracted.

Heir

Someone entitled to inherit under state default rules when there's no will. Different from beneficiary, which means someone named in a will.

Intestate

Dying without a will. The state's default rules determine who inherits.

Letters Testamentary

The court document proving you're the appointed executor. Banks, brokerages, and government agencies all require these. Get certified copies — usually $5–$20 each.

Personal Representative

Another name for executor. Used in many states as the standard term.

Probate

The court process of administering an estate. Includes validating the will, appointing the executor, supervising asset inventory and distribution, and ultimately closing the estate.

POD (Payable-on-Death)

A designation on a bank account that lets it pass directly to a named person at the owner's death — skipping probate.

Pour-over Will

A will whose main job is to direct any assets not titled in a living trust to be "poured over" into the trust during probate. Used as a safety net for assets the deceased forgot to retitle.

Residuary

Whatever is left of the estate after specific and general bequests are paid and all debts and expenses are satisfied. Goes to the "residuary beneficiary" or beneficiaries named in the will.

Right of Survivorship

A way of jointly owning property where, at the death of one owner, the survivor automatically owns the whole thing. Passes outside probate.

TOD (Transfer-on-Death)

Like POD, but for brokerage accounts and (in some states) vehicles and real estate. Asset passes directly to the named beneficiary at death, skipping probate.

Trust

A legal arrangement where one person (the trustee) holds property for the benefit of another (the beneficiary). Living trusts created during the deceased's life often hold the bulk of an estate and pass outside probate.

Will

A signed, witnessed document directing how a person's property is to be distributed at death. The court "admits" the will to probate, meaning the court accepts it as valid and authorizes the executor to follow it.

BIBLIOGRAPHY & REFERENCE GUIDE

◆

Sources, references, and further reading. State-specific rules vary materially; this list focuses on sources useful across jurisdictions.

Statutory and Procedural Sources

- Each state's Probate Code (or Estates and Trusts Code). Find your state's version at the state legislature's website. This is the canonical source for procedural rules.
- Each state's Uniform Probate Code (UPC) adoption (where applicable). About 18 states have adopted some version of the UPC, which standardizes much of the procedure.
- Your county probate court's website. Forms, fee schedules, local rules, and self-help materials are usually posted.
- Internal Revenue Code, primarily §§ 1014 (basis step-up), 2001-2058 (estate tax), 6018 (return filing), 6075 (return due date).

Practitioner Treatises

- Casner & Pennell, Estate Planning. The standard practitioner reference for technical issues.
- Frolik & Kaplan, Elder Law in a Nutshell. A practitioner's overview useful for executors dealing with end-of-life issues.
- American College of Trust and Estate Counsel (ACTEC) practice guides. Practitioner-focused, available to members of the bar.

Plain-Language Guides

- Nolo's How to Probate an Estate in California (and parallel state-specific Nolo titles for other states). Accessible, accurate, regularly updated.
- AARP's Estate Planning Survival Guide. Reader-friendly overview of the broader estate-planning landscape.
- The Complete Estate & Property Planning Series (AVOY Publishing) — institutional companion to this series, covering Trust Made Simple, Probate Explained, Property After Death, and Estate Taxes Explained.

Government and Nonprofit Resources

- IRS.gov — for EIN application, tax forms, publications. Search "deceased taxpayer" for relevant guidance.

• SSA.gov — for survivor benefits and death-reporting procedures.

• VA.gov — for veteran's benefits including burial allowance.

• USPS Mail Forwarding for Deceased — procedures for redirecting mail.

• Your state's vital records office — for ordering certified death certificates.

Online Reference

• American Bar Association's Estate Planning Information section.

• AARP's Caregiving Resource Center for guidance on the broader transition.

• Each state bar association's lawyer-referral service for finding qualified probate attorneys.

ABOUT THE PUBLISHER

AVOY Publishing is the trade imprint of AVOY, LLC. Our books are written for the intelligent reader who would rather understand a thing than be told what to think about it.

We publish in two parallel series on estate and property planning:

The Complete Estate & Property Planning Series is the institutional reference set — four books that together provide a comprehensive treatment of the legal and financial systems involved in transferring wealth at death.

The Estate Execution & Probate Series (of which this book is the first) is the practical, action-oriented companion — four books written for readers who need to *do* something, not study a system.

AVOY's editorial standard is plain language, respect for the reader's intelligence, refusal to retreat into jargon, and a commitment to telling the whole truth about subjects where incomplete answers cause real harm.

Visit us at avoyhq.com.

ABOUT THE AUTHOR

A. Perkins is a #1 Amazon bestselling author and the founder of AVOY Publishing. A former U.S. Air Force nuclear missile launch officer with an MBA, he writes for readers who would rather understand a thing than be told what to think about it.

The Executor's Practical Guide is his twenty-ninth book and the first in the Estate Execution & Probate Series.

PART

APPENDICES

Reference material for ongoing administration — return as the estate moves through its stages.

APPENDIX A — Executor at a Glance

◆

Single-page reference for what the executor does, in five lines:

1. **Find:** Identify everything the deceased owned and everything they owed.
2. **Pay:** Pay debts and taxes in priority order.
3. **Distribute:** Give what's left to the beneficiaries named in the will.
4. **Document:** Track every dollar in and out; collect signed releases.
5. **Close:** File the final accounting; receive the court's discharge order.

Average duration: 9–15 months. Average time investment: 200–400 hours.

APPENDIX B — State Probate Threshold Map

◆

Most states have a "small estate" procedure that bypasses full probate when the estate is below a certain value. Below are the approximate thresholds (verify current numbers — they change). Estates under the threshold can often be handled with a simple affidavit rather than full probate administration.

- **California:** $184,500 (small-estate affidavit available).
- **New York:** $50,000 (simplified "voluntary administration").
- **Texas:** $75,000 (small-estate affidavit; muniment of title also available).
- **Florida:** $75,000 (summary administration available); 2 years if deceased was dead more than 2 years.
- **Illinois:** $100,000 (small-estate affidavit).
- **Pennsylvania:** $50,000 (simplified procedures).
- **Ohio:** $35,000 (released from administration), or $100,000 if spouse-only.
- **Michigan:** $25,000 (small-estate affidavit).
- **Georgia:** No formal small-estate procedure for transferring real property; some flexibility for personal

property.

- **Most other states:** $50,000–$200,000, with significant variation. Verify with your county probate court.

If the estate qualifies for a small-estate procedure, full probate may not be needed at all. Check before opening a formal probate case.

APPENDIX C — The Executor's First-Sixty-Days Checklist

◆

Day-by-day priorities for the first two months.

Days 1–3

- Notify immediate family personally.
- Engage funeral home; arrange transfer of body if applicable.
- Secure home (locks, mail, perishables, thermostat).
- Photograph every room for the inventory baseline.
- Find and secure the will, keys, wallet.

Days 4–14

- Order 8–10 certified death certificates.
- Locate trust documents, beneficiary forms, account statements, deeds, insurance, loan documents.
- Tell Social Security and credit bureaus.
- Notify employer if applicable.

Days 15–30

- File petition for probate with the county court.
- Submit the will.
- Apply for the estate's EIN.

- Attend appointment hearing; receive Letters Testamentary.
- Engage a probate attorney if needed; engage a CPA who does estate work.

Days 31–60

- Open the estate bank account.
- Notify all financial institutions formally with death certificate and Letters.
- Send beneficiary notification letters.
- Publish notice to creditors; send direct notice to known creditors.
- Begin formal asset inventory.
- Get appraisals on real estate and high-value personal property.

APPENDIX D — Common Probate Forms and What They Mean

◆

Forms you'll encounter, what they're for, and where to get them.

- **Petition for Probate.** The opening filing that asks the court to admit the will and appoint you. State-specific form on the court's website.
- **Letters Testamentary (or Letters of Administration).** The court's certificate proving you're appointed. You'll need certified copies for banks and brokerages.
- **Oath of Executor.** A short signed statement promising to perform the duties faithfully. Filed at appointment.
- **Bond (if required).** A surety bond protecting the estate from executor misconduct. Many wills waive the requirement; some states waive it for family executors.
- **Notice to Creditors.** Both the newspaper publication and the direct written notice.
- **Inventory.** The formal list of estate assets with valuations. Usually due 60–90 days after appointment.
- **Petition for Approval of Final Accounting.** The closing filing along with the accounting and distribution plan.

- **Receipts and Releases.** Signed by each beneficiary acknowledging their distribution and releasing the executor.
- **Order of Discharge.** The court order that ends your role as executor.

APPENDIX E — Sample Letter to Beneficiaries

◆

Use as a starting template; adjust for your circumstances. Send by certified mail with return receipt within the first 30 days after appointment.

> **INITIAL LETTER TO BENEFICIARY**
>
> Dear [Beneficiary Name], As you may know, [Deceased] passed away on [date]. I've been named in their will as executor, and I'm writing to let you know that you are named as a beneficiary in the will. I am currently in the process of filing the will with the [County] Probate Court and asking to be formally appointed. Once the court appoints me and admits the will, you'll receive a copy of the will and a notice of your specific interest in the estate. Estate administration usually takes nine to fifteen months. During that time, I'll send periodic updates and a final accounting before any distribution is made. There's nothing you need to do right now except confirm your current mailing address and contact information. Please reach out at [email/phone] with any questions. I'll do my best to keep you informed throughout the process. With appreciation, [Your name], Executor.

APPENDIX F — Annotated Reading List for the Serious Reader

◆

If this book has been useful and you want to go deeper, these are the resources we recommend most often.

- **Nolo's Executor's Guide** by Mary Randolph. The single best general-purpose executor's handbook in print. Pairs well with this book — Nolo for procedure depth, this book for plain-language framing.
- **The American Bar Association's Guide to Wills and Estates.** Broader scope but reliable.
- **Your state-specific Nolo title.** "How to Probate an Estate in [State]" exists for most states. Tactical procedural reference.
- **The Complete Estate & Property Planning Series (AVOY Publishing).** Trust Made Simple, Probate Explained, Property After Death, Estate Taxes Explained. The institutional companion set — useful when this book's plain-language treatment leaves you wanting a deeper conceptual frame.
- **Each state bar association's lawyer-referral service.** When you need a probate attorney and don't know where to start.

APPENDIX G — The Twelve-Month Estate Calendar

◆

Month-by-month schedule for a typical estate. Treat as a default; adjust to your specific case.

- **Month 1.** Confirm death. Secure home. Find documents. Notify critical parties (Social Security, employer, credit bureaus).
- **Month 2.** File probate. Get appointed. Apply for EIN. Open estate account. Send beneficiary letters. Publish creditor notice.
- **Month 3.** Complete formal inventory. Get appraisals. Notify all financial institutions. Begin creditor-claim processing.
- **Month 4.** Continue inventory and appraisals. Begin work on final 1040 if needed. List real estate if it will be sold.
- **Month 5.** Process creditor claims; approve, deny, or negotiate. Continue tax preparation.
- **Month 6.** File deceased's final 1040 (if April 15 deadline falls here). Begin work on estate 1041 if applicable.
- **Month 7.** Close out asset sales. Finalize creditor handling.

- **Month 8.** Reconcile estate account. Begin drafting final accounting. Plan distribution.
- **Month 9.** Complete final accounting. Communicate distribution plan to beneficiaries.
- **Month 10.** Send final accounting to beneficiaries; allow 30 days for review.
- **Month 11.** File final accounting with court. Attend closing hearing or receive order. Begin distributions.
- **Month 12.** Complete distributions. Collect signed releases. File receipts. Receive order of discharge. Close estate account.

APPENDIX H — Family Communication Framework

◆

Most family conflicts during estate administration come from uneven information. Avoid them with three habits:

1. **Same message, same time, every beneficiary.** Send a single monthly update to all beneficiaries on the same day each month. Two paragraphs is enough. Status of major tasks, expected next steps, expected closing date.
2. **Defer specifics until you have facts.** "When will I get my share?" gets answered "After creditors are handled and the court approves — typically months 11–12." Not "around six months" or "as soon as possible."
3. **Document any agreement in writing.** If a beneficiary wants a specific item, get that in writing. If two beneficiaries want the same item, document the resolution in writing. Verbal agreements vanish under stress.

The structure prevents the fight. Most family fights aren't really about the silverware — they're about being heard and being treated fairly. A transparent process handles both.

APPENDIX I — Subject Index

Key topics and where to find them.

APPENDIX J — Reader's Quick-Start Guide

◆

If the death just happened and you have ten minutes, here is the absolute minimum.

Today

- Call immediate family personally.
- Call the funeral home.
- Lock the deceased's home.
- Find the will if you can.

This week

- Order 8–10 certified death certificates through the funeral home.
- Photograph every room of the home.
- Collect the important documents in one place (will, accounts, deeds, insurance, tax returns).
- Tell Social Security and the employer.

This month

- File the will with the probate court.
- Petition to be appointed executor.
- Get an EIN for the estate.

- Open the estate bank account once appointed.
- Send notification letters to beneficiaries.

When you have time, come back and read the book from Chapter 1. For now: today, this week, this month.

APPENDIX K — Chapter-by-Chapter Summary

One-paragraph summary of each chapter for fast review.

- **Chapter 1 — What Happens First.** The first 72 hours: confirm the death through the funeral home, secure the home, find the will and key documents.
- **Chapter 2 — Understanding Your Role.** The executor's job is a three-stage operation (find, pay, distribute) bound by one rule: put the estate first. You can get paid; you can decline.
- **Chapter 3 — Locating the Will.** Wills usually live in one of six places. If the original's missing, file a copy with affidavits or proceed as intestate.
- **Chapter 4 — Securing Assets.** Lock down the house, vehicles, accounts, real estate, business interests, personal property, and digital assets in the first two weeks.
- **Chapter 5 — Notifications.** Order: agencies and credit bureaus first, banks and brokerages next, beneficiaries by end of month one. In writing, with death certificates.
- **Chapter 6 — Debts.** The estate pays debts in priority order; beneficiaries don't inherit unsecured debts. Wait for formal claims before paying anything.

- **Chapter 7 — Managing Day-to-Day.** Open the estate bank account, get an EIN, run every transaction through the account, track every dollar in and out.
- **Chapter 8 — Working with Attorneys.** Hire one for the legal work, do the administrative work yourself. Know what they should and shouldn't bill you for.
- **Chapter 9 — Distribution.** Read the will carefully. Pay debts first, then specific bequests, general bequests, then residuary. Wait for the creditor window. Collect signed releases.
- **Chapter 10 — Common Mistakes.** Eleven recurring mistakes with the specific cure for each. Most are reversible if caught early.
- **Chapter 11 — Timeline.** Month-by-month playbook from death to discharge. Typical close: 9–15 months.
- **Chapter 12 — Final Checklist.** The closing accounting, the discharge order, the 20-item one-page closing checklist.

APPENDIX L — The Complete AVOY Library

Recommended reading order across all eight books

◆

AVOY publishes two parallel four-book series on estate and property planning. Together they form the complete library — one institutional/educational set and one practical/action-oriented set — and they're designed to work together.

Here is the recommended reading order, depending on where you are.

Continue Your Estate Planning Journey

Start with the fundamentals

Trust Made Simple — The first book in *The Complete Estate & Property Planning Series*. The conceptual foundation: what a trust is, when to use one, and how it interacts with the rest of the estate-planning toolkit. Read this first if you're starting from scratch on the planning side.

Then take action

The Executor's Practical Guide *(this volume)* — Book 1 of the *Estate Execution & Probate Series*. The practical step-by-step for the person who has been named as executor and needs to know what to do, in what order, today and tomorrow.

Probate Made Simple — Book 2 of *Estate Execution & Probate*. The companion to this book that focuses specifically on the court process — navigating filings, deadlines, hearings, and the formal procedural side of administration.

Protect your estate

How to Avoid Probate — Book 3 of *Estate Execution & Probate*. The prevention angle. Trusts, beneficiary designations, joint titling, TOD/POD accounts, and the structures that keep an estate out of court entirely. Read this for your own planning.

Stay organized

Estate Planning Checklist — Book 4 of *Estate Execution & Probate*. The fillable workbook for organizing your own estate so that whoever administers it for you has it easier than you did. The action-format complement to *Trust Made Simple*.

Deepen your understanding

Three additional volumes in *The Complete Estate & Property Planning Series* complete the institutional set:

- **Probate Explained** *(Book 2)* — The comprehensive treatment of probate as a legal procedure. The institutional companion to *Probate Made Simple* in the action series.
- **Property After Death** *(Book 3)* — How real estate and other property transitions to heirs. Co-tenancy, partition, real-estate transfer, ancillary probate.
- **Estate Taxes Explained** *(Book 4)* — The federal and state transfer-tax system, the basis-step-up, and the eight recurring surprise patterns. Critical for estates with substantial assets.

How the Two Series Fit Together

Each book in each series is designed to stand alone. Read any single book and you'll have a complete picture of its topic.

Read paired books across the two series and you'll have the full picture — the conceptual *and* the practical:

- **Probate Made Simple** + **Probate Explained** — the action playbook plus the institutional reference for probate as a legal process.
- **The Executor's Practical Guide** + **Trust Made Simple** — what to do when you've been named executor plus the planning that creates better executors' jobs.
- **How to Avoid Probate** + **Property After Death** — the avoidance toolkit plus the institutional treatment of what happens when avoidance doesn't apply.

- **Estate Planning Checklist + Estate Taxes Explained** — the workbook for organizing your affairs plus the comprehensive tax reference for estates with substantial assets.

Eight books. Two complementary perspectives. One coherent library of American estate and property planning. Visit avoyhq.com for the full catalog and current pricing.

"Predictable is the most valuable thing an institution can be at the moments when families have the least capacity to handle surprise."

A FINAL WORD

◆

Being executor is one of the more difficult things adult life will ask of you. You probably didn't volunteer. Someone you cared about chose you, and you said yes because saying yes felt like loyalty.

You read a book. You took notes. You opened bank accounts and filed papers and made phone calls and sent letters and wrote checks and sat through hearings and signed receipts. Through all of it, you put the estate first.

That is a real thing to have done.

Whatever measure of thanks you receive — and the thanks tend to be quiet — the work itself is the answer to whether it mattered. The people who inherited what was supposed to be theirs inherited it because you made sure they did. The creditors got paid in the right order. The court signed the discharge.

The financial life of someone you loved was wound down with care by someone they trusted.

Take what you learned and use it twice. Use it now, in the weeks after the discharge, to rest. And use it later, quietly, for your own affairs — so that the person you name as your own executor has it easier than you did.

Take care of yours.

— AVOY Publishing

Spring 2026

APPENDIX M — When the Estate Has a Business

◆

Business interests add complexity. This appendix is a short field guide for executors who inherit one.

First: locate the operating documents

If the business is a corporation, you want the articles of incorporation, the bylaws, the shareholder agreement, any buy-sell agreement, the most recent meeting minutes, and the most recent balance sheet and tax return. If it's an LLC, you want the operating agreement and the same financial documents.

If it's a sole proprietorship or general partnership, you want the partnership agreement (if any), the most recent Schedule C or partnership return, and any business bank statements.

Second: locate the buy-sell agreement, if any

Most well-structured businesses have a buy-sell agreement among the owners. The agreement specifies what happens at an owner's death — typically a forced sale of the deceased owner's interest at a pre-agreed valuation method, often funded by life insurance the business carried on each owner.

If there's a buy-sell, the agreement runs the show. The deceased's interest is sold to the surviving owners (or the company itself), the estate receives the agreed purchase price, and the executor's job is to verify the transaction is correctly executed and the proceeds reach the estate account.

Third: if there's no buy-sell

The deceased's interest passes through the estate under the will. The executor has the deceased's voting and management rights until distribution to the beneficiaries. This is where things get complicated — especially in closely-held businesses where the surviving owners and the beneficiaries have different interests.

Get specialized counsel. The probate attorney handling the estate often is not the right person for the business side. You may need a business attorney, a CPA who works with closely-held businesses, and a business-valuation specialist.

Fourth: keep the business running

While the estate is open, the business has to continue operating. Customers still need to be served. Employees still need to be paid. Vendors still need to be managed. The executor — or an interim manager the executor appoints — has to keep the lights on.

Most family businesses survive an owner's death because someone steps in to manage during the transition. Most businesses that fail after an owner's death do so because no one did.

APPENDIX O — 50-State Probate Quick Reference

◆

Each state runs probate slightly differently. The thresholds and procedures below are accurate at time of writing — verify current numbers with your county probate court before relying on them. The categories: small-estate threshold (under which a simplified affidavit usually substitutes for full probate), and typical full-probate timeline (which assumes an uncontested estate in the most common configuration).

Alabama

Small-estate threshold: $32,047 (indexed). Typical timeline: 9–12 months. Inheritance tax: none. Notable: requires the will to be filed within 5 years of death.

Alaska

Small-estate threshold: $50,000 personal property, $100,000 vehicles. Typical timeline: 6–12 months. Inheritance tax: none. UPC state.

Arizona

Small-estate threshold: $75,000 personal property, $100,000 real property. Typical timeline: 6–9 months. Inheritance tax: none. UPC state.

Arkansas

Small-estate threshold: $100,000. Typical timeline: 9–12 months. Inheritance tax: none.

California

Small-estate threshold: $184,500 (indexed). Typical timeline: 9–18 months. Inheritance tax: none. Notable: significant statutory fees for executor and attorney based on estate size.

Colorado

Small-estate threshold: $74,000. Typical timeline: 6–12 months. Inheritance tax: none. UPC state.

Connecticut

Small-estate threshold: $40,000. Typical timeline: 12–18 months. State estate tax: yes (above ~$13M federal threshold).

Delaware

Small-estate threshold: $30,000. Typical timeline: 8–12 months. Inheritance tax: none.

Florida

Small-estate threshold: $75,000, or 2 years post-death regardless of size. Typical timeline: 6–12 months. Inheritance tax: none. Notable: "summary administration" available, and homestead has special rules.

Georgia

Small-estate threshold: none (no formal small-estate affidavit for real property). Typical timeline: 6–12 months. Inheritance tax: none.

Hawaii

Small-estate threshold: $100,000. Typical timeline: 8–12 months. State estate tax: yes (threshold around $5.5M).

Idaho

Small-estate threshold: $100,000. Typical timeline: 6–9 months. Inheritance tax: none. UPC state.

Illinois

Small-estate threshold: $100,000. Typical timeline: 9–15 months. State estate tax: yes (threshold $4M).

Indiana

Small-estate threshold: $100,000. Typical timeline: 6–12 months. Inheritance tax: none (repealed 2013).

Iowa

Small-estate threshold: $50,000. Typical timeline: 9–12 months. Inheritance tax: yes (varies by beneficiary class).

Kansas

Small-estate threshold: $40,000. Typical timeline: 9–12 months. Inheritance tax: none.

Kentucky

Small-estate threshold: $30,000. Typical timeline: 9–18 months. Inheritance tax: yes (varies by beneficiary class).

Louisiana

Small-estate threshold: $125,000. Typical timeline: 9–15 months. Inheritance tax: none. Notable: civil-law system; "succession" rather than probate.

Maine

Small-estate threshold: $40,000. Typical timeline: 6–12 months. State estate tax: yes (threshold $6.4M). UPC state.

Maryland

Small-estate threshold: $50,000, or $100,000 spouse-only. Typical timeline: 9–12 months. State estate and inheritance tax: yes (both).

Massachusetts

Small-estate threshold: $25,000 plus a car. Typical timeline: 9–15 months. State estate tax: yes (threshold $2M).

Michigan

Small-estate threshold: $25,000. Typical timeline: 6–12 months. Inheritance tax: none. UPC state.

Minnesota

Small-estate threshold: $75,000. Typical timeline: 6–12 months. State estate tax: yes (threshold $3M). UPC state.

Mississippi

Small-estate threshold: $75,000. Typical timeline: 9–12 months. Inheritance tax: none.

Missouri

Small-estate threshold: $40,000. Typical timeline: 9–12 months. Inheritance tax: none.

Montana

Small-estate threshold: $50,000. Typical timeline: 6–12 months. Inheritance tax: none. UPC state.

Nebraska

Small-estate threshold: $50,000. Typical timeline: 6–12 months. Inheritance tax: yes (varies by beneficiary class). UPC state.

Nevada

Small-estate threshold: $100,000, or $25,000 personal property. Typical timeline: 6–12 months. Inheritance tax: none.

New Hampshire

Small-estate threshold: $10,000 personal property. Typical timeline: 9–12 months. Inheritance tax: none.

New Jersey

Small-estate threshold: $50,000 (spouse), $20,000 (other). Typical timeline: 9–15 months. Inheritance tax: yes (varies by beneficiary class).

New Mexico

Small-estate threshold: $50,000. Typical timeline: 6–12 months. Inheritance tax: none. UPC state.

New York

Small-estate threshold: $50,000. Typical timeline: 12–18 months. State estate tax: yes (threshold $7M). Notable: "voluntary administration" simplified procedure available.

North Carolina

Small-estate threshold: $20,000, or $30,000 spouse-only. Typical timeline: 9–12 months. Inheritance tax: none.

North Dakota

Small-estate threshold: $50,000. Typical timeline: 6–12 months. Inheritance tax: none. UPC state.

Ohio

Small-estate threshold: $35,000, or $100,000 spouse-only. Typical timeline: 9–12 months. Inheritance tax: none (repealed 2013).

Oklahoma

Small-estate threshold: $50,000. Typical timeline: 9–12 months. Inheritance tax: none.

Oregon

Small-estate threshold: $75,000 personal property, $200,000 real property. Typical timeline: 6–12 months. State estate tax: yes (threshold $1M, low).

Pennsylvania

Small-estate threshold: $50,000. Typical timeline: 9–15 months. Inheritance tax: yes (varies by beneficiary class).

Rhode Island

Small-estate threshold: $15,000. Typical timeline: 9–15 months. State estate tax: yes (threshold ~$1.7M).

South Carolina

Small-estate threshold: $25,000. Typical timeline: 9–12 months. Inheritance tax: none.

South Dakota

Small-estate threshold: $50,000. Typical timeline: 6–12 months. Inheritance tax: none. UPC state.

Tennessee

Small-estate threshold: $50,000. Typical timeline: 6–12 months. Inheritance tax: none (repealed 2016).

Texas

Small-estate threshold: $75,000. Typical timeline: 6–9 months. Inheritance tax: none. Notable: "independent administration" with minimal court supervision available.

Utah

Small-estate threshold: $100,000. Typical timeline: 6–12 months. Inheritance tax: none. UPC state.

Vermont

Small-estate threshold: $45,000. Typical timeline: 9–12 months. Inheritance tax: none.

Virginia

Small-estate threshold: $50,000. Typical timeline: 9–12 months. Inheritance tax: none.

Washington

Small-estate threshold: $100,000. Typical timeline: 6–12 months. State estate tax: yes (threshold $2.2M).

West Virginia

Small-estate threshold: $50,000. Typical timeline: 9–12 months. Inheritance tax: none.

Wisconsin

Small-estate threshold: $50,000. Typical timeline: 9–12 months. Inheritance tax: none.

Wyoming

Small-estate threshold: $200,000. Typical timeline: 6–9 months. Inheritance tax: none.

District of Columbia

Small-estate threshold: $40,000. Typical timeline: 12–18 months. State estate tax: yes (threshold $4.5M).

Cross-state notes

If the deceased owned real property in more than one state, an "ancillary probate" proceeding is usually required in each state where they owned property. The primary state is the state of legal residence; ancillary states handle only the real property in their boundaries. Each ancillary proceeding has its own attorney, fees, and timeline.

Real estate in multiple states is one of the leading causes of timeline extension beyond 15 months.

Inheritance tax states (Iowa, Kentucky, Maryland, Nebraska, New Jersey, Pennsylvania) apply tax based on the beneficiary's relationship to the deceased. Spouses and lineal descendants are usually exempt or taxed at low rates; siblings and unrelated beneficiaries are taxed at higher rates. The executor withholds the tax from each beneficiary's distribution and remits to the state.

Verify all of the above with the specific county probate court before relying on it. These figures change regularly through state legislation.

APPENDIX N — Taking Care of Yourself

◆

Most books about being an executor don't include this appendix. They should.

You are doing one of the more difficult things adult life asks of a person. You are managing a complex multi-month project. You are also grieving. The combination is harder than either alone.

Six things that help

One: pace the work. This is a nine-to-fifteen-month project, not a sprint. The first month is exhausting; months 4–9 are steady; the closing months ramp again. Build in rest days. Take real weekends. The work will still be there Monday.

Two: ask for help with the parts you don't have to do alone. A family member can pick up mail. A friend can drive to the bank. A neighbor can walk through the empty house. The legal work is yours; the operational support doesn't have to be.

Three: protect your own life. Your job, your kids, your marriage, your health — these don't pause for the estate. If the estate work is crowding out everything else, something is wrong with how you've structured it. Step back, ask what can be deferred, and rebalance.

Four: keep a paper journal. Not the official accounting — a personal log. What you did this week. How you felt about it. What you're worried about. The act of writing things down protects you twice: it preserves details you might forget, and it lets the work live outside your head, where it isn't running on a loop.

Five: notice the small wins. The bank account opened. The first creditor claim resolved. The inventory filed. Each of these is a real accomplishment. Don't wait until the discharge to acknowledge progress. Notice it weekly.

Six: at the end, rest. Don't immediately take on another big project. Don't volunteer for someone else's estate. Give yourself a season of quiet. You've earned it.

The hard parts are real

Being an executor is grief work disguised as paperwork. The same files that prove the estate is closing also remind you, every day, of who is gone. Some days the paperwork will land harder than other days. That's not a sign you're doing it wrong; it's a sign you loved the person who chose you.

Let it land. Take the day if you need to. The estate will keep until tomorrow.

APPENDIX P — Sample Letters and Templates

◆

Use these as starting templates. Adjust for your circumstances. None of these are legal forms — they are plain communications you'll send to beneficiaries, creditors, and institutions during administration.

Template 1 — Initial Notice to Beneficiary

> **INITIAL NOTICE TO BENEFICIARY**
>
> Dear [Name], As you may know, [Deceased] passed away on [date]. I've been named in their will as executor, and I'm writing to let you know you are named as a beneficiary. I'm in the process of filing the will with the [County] Probate Court. Once I am formally appointed and the will is admitted, you will receive a copy of the will and a notice of your specific interest. Estate administration usually takes nine to fifteen months. I'll send periodic updates. Please confirm your current mailing address. With appreciation, [Executor name].

Template 2 — Monthly Beneficiary Update

> **MONTHLY BENEFICIARY UPDATE**
>
> Dear [Beneficiaries], A brief update on the estate of [Deceased] for [Month]. Completed this month: [list of tasks — e.g., "received Letters Testamentary," "completed asset inventory," "paid creditor claims for X and Y," "filed deceased's final 1040"]. Coming next: [list of upcoming items]. Expected closing date: still tracking to [month/year]. Please let me know if you have questions. With appreciation, [Executor name].

Template 3 — Notice of Death to Creditor

NOTICE OF DEATH TO CREDITOR

Dear [Creditor], This letter provides formal notice that [Deceased], your account holder under account number [number], passed away on [date]. A copy of the certified death certificate is enclosed. The estate is being administered through the [County] Probate Court under case number [case number]. All claims against the estate must be presented in writing to the executor at the address below within [state-specific window]. Claims not timely presented may be barred. Please direct future correspondence to: [Executor name, address]. Sincerely, [Executor name].

Template 4 — Denial of Creditor Claim

DENIAL OF CREDITOR CLAIM

Dear [Creditor], I am in receipt of your claim dated [date] in the amount of [$amount] against the estate of [Deceased]. After review, the claim is denied for the following reason: [specific reason — e.g., "the underlying obligation is not supported by documentation," "the claim was filed after the statutory deadline," "the obligation was satisfied prior to death"]. You have [state-specific period] to contest this denial by filing with the [County] Probate Court. Sincerely, [Executor name].

Template 5 — Distribution Notice

DISTRIBUTION NOTICE

Dear [Beneficiary], The estate is approaching closing. Your final distribution under the terms of the will is [specific items, dollar amount, or both]. I propose to deliver this on or about [date], which is [30+] days from this letter. Before delivery, I'll need you to sign the enclosed Receipt and Release acknowledging your distribution and releasing the estate from further claims. If you have any questions or wish to discuss the final accounting (enclosed), please contact me by [date]. With appreciation, [Executor name].

Template 6 — Receipt and Release

> **RECEIPT AND RELEASE FORM**
>
> I, [Beneficiary Name], acknowledge receipt of [specific distribution] from the Estate of [Deceased], representing my full share under the terms of the will dated [date]. I have reviewed the final accounting and approve it. I release the executor, [Executor Name], from any further claims arising from the administration of this estate. Dated: [date]. Signed: ______________________________ [Beneficiary Name].

Template 7 — Final Thank-You Note

> **FINAL THANK-YOU NOTE**
>
> Dear [Beneficiaries], The estate of [Deceased] has been closed. The court has signed the order of discharge. Thank you for your patience throughout this process. Please retain your copy of the final accounting and the receipt and release for your records. With appreciation, [Executor name].

When to Adapt

These templates are starting points. Adjust the tone for your specific family. Some families want more warmth; others want crisp efficiency. Read the room. What matters is that every template (1) contains the factual information required, (2) maintains a respectful tone, and (3) creates a documented record. The specific words can move.

APPENDIX Q — Words and Phrases You'll Hear

◆

Beyond the Glossary at the front of this book, these are the phrases you'll hear from lawyers, courts, and financial institutions — often spoken quickly, often without explanation, often when you need to make a decision right then. Each entry is what the phrase actually means in practice, in plain words.

"Abatement"

What happens when the estate doesn't have enough to pay all the bequests the will provides. Specific bequests get paid first; if money runs out, general bequests get reduced proportionally. Most wills include language directing how abatement should be handled.

"Ademption"

What happens when a specific bequest no longer exists at the time of death. "I leave my Tesla to my nephew" — but the Tesla was sold a year before death. The nephew gets nothing in place of the Tesla. The bequest is "adeemed."

"Ancillary probate"

A separate probate proceeding in a state where the deceased owned real property but was not a resident. The primary probate happens in the state of residence; ancillary probates happen in each other state where real property sat. Each has its own attorney, fees, and timeline.

"Apparent intent"

The court's reading of what the deceased intended, even where the will's words are unclear. Comes up most when a will is poorly drafted or when circumstances have changed since the will was signed.

"Bond"

A surety bond protecting the estate from executor misconduct. The bond is purchased from a surety company; the cost is typically 0.5% of estate value. Many wills waive the bond. Many states waive it for family executors.

"By representation"

A way of distributing inheritance when a beneficiary predeceased the deceased. Example: a will leaves one-third each to three children. If one child died before the parent, that child's one-third is divided "by representation" among that child's own children.

"Codicil"

A formal amendment to a will. Treated as a mini-will for validity purposes. Usually used to make small changes without rewriting the entire will.

"Convey"

Transfer ownership, typically of real estate. "Convey the property to the trust" means transfer title.

"Devise"

A gift of real property in a will. ("Bequest" is personal property; "devise" is real property. Both kinds are referred to as gifts under the will.)

"DPOA / Durable power of attorney"

A document giving someone authority to act for the principal financially. "Durable" means it survives the principal's incapacity. It ends at death — once death occurs, only the executor has authority.

"Escheat"

What happens to an estate when there's no will and no living relatives close enough to inherit under intestate rules. The estate passes to the state. Rare in practice.

"Estate income tax"

Different from estate transfer tax. Estate income tax (Form 1041) applies to income earned by the estate during administration — interest, dividends, rental income, capital gains on sales. Filed annually while the estate is open.

"Per capita" / "Per stirpes"

Two different ways to divide an inheritance. "Per capita" means equal shares among living beneficiaries in the same generation. "Per stirpes" means by branch — if a child has died, that child's share passes intact to their children. The will usually specifies which method applies.

"Pretermitted heir"

A child of the deceased who isn't mentioned in the will — usually because they were born after the will was signed. Many states have laws protecting pretermitted heirs by giving them a share equivalent to what they'd get under intestate succession.

"Settle"

Close out, in estate context. "Settle the estate" means complete the administration and close the case.

"Sound mind"

Mental capacity sufficient to make a valid will. The deceased must have known they were making a will, understood roughly what they owned, and known who their family was. Capacity challenges are a common will-contest ground.

"Spendthrift clause"

A trust provision preventing a beneficiary from transferring or assigning their share of the trust to creditors. Common in trusts for beneficiaries with poor judgment about money or vulnerability to creditor claims.

"Testator" / "Testatrix"

The person who made the will. Testator is the general term; testatrix is the older female form, rarely used today.

"Undue influence"

A will-contest ground claiming someone manipulated the deceased into changing their will to benefit the manipulator. Hard to prove. More commonly alleged when a late-life will dramatically favors a recent caregiver over longstanding family.

APPENDIX S — Selling the Family Home

◆

More estates than not include a house. More often than not, the house has to be sold during administration — because no single beneficiary wants it, because the estate needs cash to pay debts, or because the will directs sale. The home is usually the single largest asset in the estate. Getting the sale right matters.

This appendix is the playbook for selling the family home while the estate is open. It's a longer-form appendix because the topic warrants it. Read it before you list.

Step 1 — Confirm you have authority to sell

You cannot sign a listing agreement or a deed without authority. Authority comes from one of three places: the will explicitly granting the executor a power of sale, the court granting authority via the Letters Testamentary, or a specific court order authorizing the sale.

Check the will first. Most modern wills grant the executor a broad power of sale ("my executor shall have full power to sell any property of the estate without further authorization"). If the will is silent or restrictive, consult the probate attorney before listing.

Some states require a separate court petition to sell real estate even when the will grants the power; others let the executor proceed on the strength of Letters alone.

Step 2 — Get the property ready

Before you list, do four things at the house:

1. **Clean it out.** This is emotionally hard but practically essential. Photographs of family members in every room, personal items in every drawer, a quarter-century of accumulated possessions in the basement — none of it helps the sale. Hire a local moving company to pack personal property; identify what beneficiaries want kept; store the rest in a single off-site storage unit during the sale window.

2. **Make repairs that don't require permits.** Replace burned-out bulbs. Fix dripping faucets. Patch wall holes. Repaint scuffed walls. Steam-clean carpets. Buyers notice deferred maintenance and assume there's more they can't see.

3. **Do not make major upgrades.** Don't renovate the kitchen. Don't replace the roof unless it's actively leaking. Renovations rarely return their cost in the sale, and they extend the timeline.

4. **Get a pre-listing inspection.** Cost: $400–$800. The inspection tells you what's wrong before the buyer's

inspector tells them. You can either fix the issues or disclose them upfront — either way, you avoid the renegotiation phase where a buyer uses the inspection to extract a price reduction.

Step 3 — Price it correctly

Get a written appraisal from a licensed appraiser ($400–$800). Get two or three comparative market analyses from local realtors (free, takes about an hour each). The numbers will vary; the right price is usually in the upper third of the realtor estimates and at or slightly below the appraisal.

Overpricing is the most common mistake. A house priced too high sits on the market for months and ends up selling for less than a correctly priced house would have. The first two weeks of a listing produce the most showings; if those two weeks pass without serious offers, the listing goes stale and serious buyers move on.

Step 4 — Hire the right agent

Interview at least three. Ask each:

- How many homes have you sold in this neighborhood in the last twelve months?
- What's your average days-on-market vs. the local average?
- What's your sale-price-to-list-price ratio?

- How do you market the property — MLS only, or also social media, open houses, broker tours?
- What's your commission, and what does it cover?

Pick the agent who answers specifically, not generically. "My average is 12 days on market vs. 27 for the area, and I closed 11 homes within a mile of this address last year" is the right kind of answer. "I specialize in this market" is not.

Step 5 — Disclose what you know — and what you don't

The estate is in a unique position with respect to seller disclosures. You, as executor, often don't know the history of the house — when the roof was replaced, whether the basement ever flooded, whether the foundation has settled.

Most states require the seller to disclose known defects, but allow the executor of an estate to disclose only what they personally know.

Use this. Honest "I don't know" answers on the seller disclosure form are legally protective. They tell the buyer to do their own inspection and remove the basis for later lawsuits over undisclosed defects.

Do disclose anything you do know — recent water damage, code issues, neighborhood disputes, anything material that you've personally observed or learned. Disclosure is the executor's friend; non-disclosure of known issues is the fastest way to be sued personally after the sale.

Step 6 — Handle multiple offers carefully

When you receive more than one offer, do not just take the highest. Consider:

- **Financing.** A cash offer at $5,000 below an offer with a 90% mortgage is often the better deal — cash closes faster and doesn't depend on the buyer's lender approving the property.
- **Contingencies.** An offer contingent on the buyer selling their existing home is weaker than a non-contingent offer at the same price.
- **Closing timeline.** A 30-day close is faster than a 60-day close. Faster closings reduce estate carrying costs.
- **Earnest money.** Higher earnest money signals a more committed buyer.
- **Inspection terms.** Some offers waive the inspection contingency entirely. Treat those skeptically — but if the buyer has done a pre-offer inspection, they're a strong buyer.

Step 7 — Close cleanly

Once you've accepted an offer, the closing is a four-week process. The buyer's lender appraises the property, the title company runs a title search, the buyer's inspector examines the property, and the closing attorney prepares the deed and the closing statement.

Two things to watch for:

- **Title issues.** If the deed isn't already in the estate's name, the title company will require a probate-administration document chain — a copy of the will, the Letters Testamentary, the order admitting the will. Get these to the title company in week 1, not week 3.
- **Appraisal gap.** If the lender's appraisal comes in below the contract price, the buyer's loan amount drops. The buyer either covers the gap in cash, renegotiates the price, or walks away. Be prepared to negotiate.

Step 8 — Deposit proceeds and distribute

At closing, the closing attorney wires the net proceeds (sale price minus mortgage payoff, real estate commission, title insurance, transfer taxes, prorated property tax) to the estate's bank account. Confirm receipt before signing anything that releases the property.

From this point, the proceeds are estate assets like any other. They're available to pay creditors, taxes, and eventually beneficiaries — in the priority order described in Chapter 6.

Special cases

A beneficiary wants to buy the house. Allowed, but with an arm's-length appraisal and ideally the written consent of every other beneficiary. The price should be the appraised value, not a discount. Document everything.

The house is in a trust. If the property is titled in the deceased's living trust, the trustee (not the executor) handles the sale — though the executor often is also the trustee. The procedures are similar but operate under the trust agreement rather than the probate court.

The house has tenants. If the deceased rented out the property, the tenants stay through the closing (subject to their lease) and the buyer inherits the lease. You'll need to provide the buyer with the lease, the security-deposit amount, and the rent payment history.

The house won't sell at any reasonable price. Distribute it in-kind to a willing beneficiary at the appraised value, treating the value as part of their share. Or, with court permission, lower the price below the appraisal and accept the smaller estate.

Selling the family home is one of the more emotional events of an estate administration. The structure above doesn't change that. But it does prevent the financial side from compounding the emotional side. Move methodically. Keep records. Defer until appointed. Document everything.

APPENDIX R — When the Estate Has a Will Contest

◆

Most wills are not contested. The ones that are tend to follow a few specific patterns, and the patterns are worth knowing — both so you can spot one early and so you can keep doing your job while litigation runs in parallel.

What a will contest actually is

A will contest is a formal legal proceeding challenging the validity of a will. It happens inside the probate court, as a separate matter from the main administration. The challenger has to prove specific grounds — usually lack of capacity, undue influence, fraud, or improper execution. The burden is on the challenger; the will is presumed valid.

The four common patterns

Late-life will favoring a new beneficiary. A will rewritten in the last six months of life, dramatically increasing the share going to a recent caregiver, neighbor, or new relationship. This pattern triggers undue-influence challenges from longstanding family members who were displaced.

Capacity at execution. A will signed when the deceased was already cognitively impaired by dementia, medication, or terminal illness. Witnesses to the signing become important. So do medical records from the weeks around execution.

Disinheritance of a child without explanation. A will that cuts out one child entirely, especially without an explanation, often triggers a contest. Many estate-planning attorneys include a short paragraph explaining the disinheritance precisely to head this off. Wills without that paragraph are easier targets.

Execution defects. A will not properly witnessed, not properly notarized (where required), missing pages, or showing signs of post-signing alteration. Procedural defects are the most easily proven contest ground but the least frequently raised.

What to do as executor

If a contest is filed, your job is not to fight it personally. Hire a probate attorney experienced in will contests if you don't already have one. The attorney represents the estate, not the beneficiaries. Your role is to provide documents, sit for depositions if asked, and continue routine administration of the estate's non-contested aspects.

Most contests settle. Litigated probate disputes are expensive and emotionally exhausting, and most parties end up at the bargaining table after the discovery phase reveals what the facts actually look like. Settlement usually involves a renegotiation of shares among the beneficiaries, signed off by the court.

What this costs the estate

Will contests are expensive. Defending one routinely costs the estate $20,000–$100,000 in attorney fees, depending on length and complexity. The estate pays these fees from estate assets, which means the ultimate beneficiaries — even the ones who didn't challenge — bear the cost.

This is why most beneficiaries, after a candid conversation with their own counsel, prefer to negotiate. Litigation rarely makes anyone whole.

Made in United States
Cleveland, OH
31 October 2026

47115102R00142